Voicelust

University of Nebraska Press: Lincoln & London

Edited by Allen Wier and Don Hendrie Jr.

Eight Contemporary Fiction Writers on Style

Voicelust

The paper in this book meets
the guidelines for permanence
and durability of the Committee
on Production Guidelines for
Book Longevity of the Council
on Library Resources

Library of Congress Cataloging
in Publication Data

Main entry under title:

Voicelust : eight contemporary
fiction writers on style.

Papers presented at the 10th
Alabama Symposium on English
& American Literature, The
Autonomous Voice: Encounters
with Style in Contemporary
Fiction, held at the University
of Alabama in 1983.
1. Fiction – Technique –
Congresses.   2. Style,
Literary – Congresses. I.
Wier, Allen, 1946–   .
II. Hendrie, Don, Jr., 1942.
III. Alabama Symposium on
English and American
Literature (10th : 1983 :
University of Alabama)
PN3383.S79V65   1985
808.3   84-25721
ISBN 0-8032-2333-1   (alk. paper)

Acknowledgments

The editors of this volume offer thanks to the following organizations and individuals: to the trustees of the University of Alabama, and in particular to President Joab Thomas; to the Office of Academic Affairs; to the Division of Continuing Studies for its logistic support of the Tenth Alabama Symposium on English and American Literature; to Douglas E. Jones, dean of the School of Arts & Sciences; to the Department of English; and to the National Endowment for the Arts. The symposium itself would have been a lesser event without the participation of Dean Jones and Professors Claudia Johnson, Elizabeth Meese, Charlotte Mears, Michael Alley, George Wolfe, and John P. Hermann. Students in the University's M.F.A. program in creative writing performed feats of care and transport with memorable spirit.

Voicelust

Sentiment is always vulnerable; when the fictional voice deliberately seeks to move you, it is an unguarded and completely exposed voice. It is easy to feel intellectually superior to such a voice. It is easy to assume that a book is a creation of and for the *mind*. And was it ever in good taste (intellectually) to encourage emotional responses—or worse, to be guided through a book by emotional responses? But a great writer guides you from one emotional response to another; a great writer isn't careful (he's not worried about offending your good taste). —John Irving

. . . art is always a meditation upon external reality rather than a representation of external reality. . . . Twenty years ago I was much more convinced of the autonomy of the literary object than I am now, and even wrote a rather persuasive defense of the proposition that I have just rejected, that the object is itself world.
—Donald Barthelme

I cannot transfer late and be at home in the tribe that knows literature as semantics, sees the Sistine Chapel as paint, hears Beethoven's Ninth as sound vibrations, and loves a lover as an appealing cellular mass; but, since all these statements are *true,* I can appreciate literature that from similar premises achieves particular styles.
—Doris Betts

Introduction

A Gathering of Voices

Trust the tale, not the teller, we know. And yet, perhaps because of the intimacy a reader shares with the writer of a work of fiction, we have a special interest in what the writer is willing to reveal about that work. Where did he get the *idea* for the story? Why did she choose *this character* to narrate the story? What does the scene on page seventeen *really mean*? Like good investigative reporters, we want to get our information from the original, the most authoritative, the true source. We want the facts. Is it a *true story*? We respect experience. And, up to a point, we respect the author's authority. Of course, depending on what the writer tells us, we reserve the right to declare that he is not necessarily the *best* source. Even when he doesn't tell us what we want or what we expect, we will take his views into consideration (though we may agree with John Barth that "a gifted writer is likely to rise above what he takes to be his aesthetic principles"). Owing to his vested interest in his work, and because of his rhetorical skills, the novelist's theories about fiction writing are usually lively, sometimes as entertaining as his fiction.

I took the long way to style: I didn't take the advice of the muse to look in my heart and write: I went to school. There I learned that the novel was dead. I learned that it had been a loose baggy monster and that someone had finally shot it up. I guess it was a whole group of hunters, the new critics. They sniffed it out and

1

gunned it down. They really had no choice, you see, because early in the century Henry James had labeled it and James Joyce had undressed it and D. H. Lawrence had sodomized it. So the new critics had to take it out of its misery.—Max Apple

The point is that real style is very hard to do. And it gets harder and harder all the time. Everybody keeps jumping in and trying to get into the act. For instance, all the good shiny prestige words keep getting snatched up by politicians and newspaper writers and cheap and grubby advertising types. Why, those people can take anything, even a nice, clean, crisp, ordinary word, one that we all know and love and use all the time, and in no time at all it will be filthy and soiled beyond any saving. — George Garrett

Those of us who were listeners in our early literary experiences, participants in the magic between oral storyteller and audience, know the pleasures (or displeasures) possible in the recognition of a familiar voice. Through the closed French doors we still know the murmured cadences of Grandmama's storytelling voice; over the slap of windshield wipers and the static of the car radio the familiar rhythms of Daddy's narrative style reach us on the backseat. Even deep in sleep, lost in nightmare, we hear our gravel-throated, mean Uncle and realize, *I'd know that voice anywhere.* We may not hear clearly—through the French doors, over the wipers, or in the depths of dream—*what* is said, but we recognize what's important: *how* it is said.

The suggestion that we use the language of ordinary men is a good one, normally, not simply because we shall reach the ear and understanding of ordinary men that way (which remains unlikely), but because such words are rich with history, both in our life and in theirs, and shine throughout with smoothness like stones that have, for vast ages, been tossed back and forth in the surf of some ancient shore, becoming eloquent, as pebbles made the mouth of Demosthenes hiss and seethe and roar. —William Gass

Art is not difficult because it wishes to be difficult, rather because it wishes to be art. However much the writer might long to be, in his work, simple, honest, straightforward, these virtues are no longer available to him. He discovers that in being simple, honest, straightforward, nothing much happens: he speaks the speakable, whereas we are looking for the as-yet unspeakable, the as-yet unspoken. —Donald Barthelme

It is not easy to make clear or show connections between the personal and the public, to shape something that began somewhere in the subconscious and present it in a fully conscious way. All writers write out of their experience, conscious and subconscious. Some time ago Henry James defined the kind of experience that is intended: "Experience is never limited, and it is never complete; it is an immense sensibility, a kind of huge spider-web of the finest silken threads suspended in the chamber of consciousness, and catching every air-borne particle in its tissue. It is the very atmosphere of the mind. . . ." There is something of the maker that is not lost in a fiction made by "one of those on whom nothing is lost."

This matter of our feelings being at odds with the "facts" is one of the things that identify us as human, and not something else. Those born in a certain time and place—and how manage to be born elsewhere?—will find that cloudy, insubstantial feelings will wreak havoc with the facts. —Wright Morris

The telling of stories is the central business of all our lives. This is not a profundity; it is merely a truth so obvious that everyone except the writer seems to overlook it. —Max Apple

As fiction writers who teach in a creative writing program we are often asked to articulate what we know about the techniques of writing fiction. In the difficulty of trying to explain something we know, we often come to know it in new, sometimes better, ways. There are times when a question shapes answers, forms opinions where there were none. These opinions are not always lasting. A good deal of fiction by students in the writing program, a good deal of all contemporary fiction, eschews the depiction of events and concentrates on the revelation of the writer's particular voice. In fiction workshops the terms *voice* and *tone* come up frequently. They are crucial elements of contemporary fiction, at once specific and vague, at once clearly understood and difficult to define adequately.

Sometimes the whole process of contemporary literature seems to me to be a voyage into narcissism: in, in, down further and further into consciousness, with the writer intruding more and more into the work. —Lee Smith

When writers write about writing they are revealing the personal reasons behind their public work, forming and formalizing opinions about their relationship to the imagination and to mystery.

3

Contemporary critics speak of "recuperating" a text, suggesting an accelerated and possibly strenuous nursing back to health of a basically sickly text, very likely one that did not even know itself to be ill. I would argue that in the competing methodologies of contemporary criticism, many of them quite rich in implications, a sort of tyranny of great expectations obtains, a rage for final explanations, a refusal to allow a work the mystery that is essential to it. —Donald Barthelme

Anthropologist Mary Tew Douglas, noting that some religions contain more magic than others, calls magic a particular *style* of religion, depending on the efficacy of symbolic forms. What Douglas means is miracle and sacrament; but in my church, words and The Word were almost sub-sacraments themselves, could work wonders, could transubstantiate any old thing by the side of a red clay road. —Doris Betts

If time were blood and an executioner struck off my head now, there would be nothing left in me for a crowd to see. A drained and cured carcass only. For I have been gutted and cleaned and hung up by time like a pig in the cellar. They say— do they not?—that I have the pig's eye. Just so. . . . I can find no fault now with that. What is gossip may sometimes be poetry. —George Garrett

I believe that a novel works more magic upon a reader by moving the reader emotionally than by convincing the reader intellectually—although, of course, these pleasures needn't be exclusive. . . . I admit that I'm more interested in speaking to the spirit than to the mind. —John Irving

One idle afternoon in 1982 we were talking about the subtle and not-so-subtle ways in which a writer filters his sensibility through a narrative voice and the voices of his characters, the kinds of ventriloquism practiced by fiction writers. Out of that loose and general talk grew the notion of inviting a healthy gamut of fiction writers we both admired to come and talk about voice as they heard it. We decided to borrow George Steiner's phrase *autonomous voice* and call the tenth Alabama Symposium on English and American Literature, a three-day gathering in October 1983, "The Autonomous Voice : Encounters With Style in Contemporary Fiction." We stated our case for this event with a formal, if somewhat dry, definition of what, privately, we had begun to call *voicelust*: "Detectable in the style of every original writer is a special sensibility, a personal manner, a unique intonation—the writer's voice. The best fiction reveals the writer's presence through an autonomous voice subject only to its

4

own laws. The matter, the substance, the *it* of fiction cannot be separated from this clear and omnipresent voice."

It's no secret to anyone who's read me that the voice I love best is the narrative voice, is the storyteller's voice. I believe that narrative momentum must override description, must restrain all our pretty abilities with the language, must be more strongly felt than even necessary information. . . . —John Irving

Even the small considerations of language contribute to any writer's voice: such prosaic questions as the length of the sentences, the favored grammatical constructions, the imagery, or the lack of imagery. —Lee Smith

The eight participants responded to this statement of the symposium's theme, each in his or her particular way. Their responses, the essays you hold in your hand, reveal the various interests of the writers and do not attempt to form a collaborative statement, do not attempt to define or promote any particular critical approach, do not attempt to fulfill any design of the editors. Where collaboration occurs or design emerges it is the result of concerns that are common to eight writers who are important practitioners of the craft today, though their methods are diverse and the range of fiction they represent is wide indeed. Wright Morris published the first of his nineteen novels in 1942; Lee Smith was born in 1944, Max Apple in 1941. The work of these eight writers bears witness to the vitality and originality of the many voices that make up contemporary American fiction. Work represented here includes the traditional and the avant garde, realism and postmodernism, the plain and the fancy style, the lyrical, the meditative, the strongly narrative. Their books include limited editions and best-sellers. Each of these eight essays in its own way addresses the need, a significant aspect of the study of contemporary fiction, to promote style without neglecting substance.

My mind remembers the way trained muscles do, so when I speak and read as well as I walk and bike, then we can say that I have incorporated my language; it has become another nature, an organlike facility; and *that* language, at least, will have been invested with meaning, not merely assigned it. —William Gass

Because the contributors are all literary artists their essays are as original and as lively as their fiction. Very little editing was needed. Some changes have been made to clarify the transformation from the podium to this volume, but the essays retain their spontaneity and free-wheeling vigor. Our only claim as editors is pride in having asked these particular writers to contribute their thoughts on style and our good fortune that they were all willing to do so.

Whatever now stalks toward Bethlehem to be born, and the writer of fiction is one of those who is free to wonder, he is increasingly reluctant to join the procession. The craft of consciousness-raising is not lost, and by a few it will always be practiced, but it now appears to have the limited uses we associate with hanggliding and skydiving. In what we might describe as a shared holding operation, the contemporary writer is committed to conscience maintenance and support—to holding time-honored gains and diminishing crucial losses. —Wright Morris

Allen Wier and Don Hendrie Jr.

Doris Betts

The Fingerprint of Style

In his posthumously published book, *On Becoming a Novelist,* the late John Gardner does not mock those who ask if we writers use pen, pencil, typewriter; if we write on yellow pads or in ledgers, during morning or after dark. Such questions, Gardner says, are really about magic, about that demon W.B. (Writer's Block). They ask us to reveal to aspirants what is lucky.

So also solemn questions about literary style may conceal the magic we suspect it of containing, the way a sober top hat is exactly the right container for a rabbit. The word *style,* itself a dead metaphor, suggests Gardner's mundane pen-and-paper questions: *style,* from the stylus of pen against paper or, before that, engraving bone or metal tool in wax.

Though the means to word-magic may be mundane, in prose its power breaks through writing in what Gardner calls "hot spots or pulsations" on the page, flares of true style or revelation. Even in student fiction, he adds, "you can spot at once where the power turns on and where it turns off." To trust that this power can be summoned on demand is what makes some writers store rotting apples in their desk drawers, take long walks, punch Arnold Bennett's time clock, turn to word processors, take to drink.

An awe at the magical power of words was conditioned in me so long ago, in such a peculiar religious manner, that even an essay like this one never results from a reasoned process begun months in advance but must be, alas, a struggle for faith and rescue. Given 365 days' notice of a deadline, I will delay, then finally set forth in three, late, anxious days the way Abraham took Isaac up the mountain—tight-lipped, scared, doubtful each time that a ram is in the thicket.

I am a kissing cousin to Abraham's tribe, southern WASP branch-head division, and from halfway up my local Mt. Moriah, I live at the right height for paradox, for art/religion, magic/reality, word and world, the tribe and the individual. Good style may be what makes good writers of every tribal affiliation—be it romantic, nihilist, religious, whatever. The style of a good writer's work is distinctive enough to be parodied; it is his individual sign, or "fingerprint of style," or what Wright Morris has called "spoor traces."

First, these clues to the tribe I know best:

Mostly Scotch-Irish, with a featherweight of Cherokee. Farmers, beauticians, policemen, millworkers, squirrel hunters, army privates. Earthy, joking people without college degrees, often without high school diplomas, living hard in piedmont North Carolina—red clay, red rivers. Use-it-up, wear-it-out, make-it-do people. Thrifty, stubborn, honest, hot-tempered. Their occasional fistfights were over money or sex but rarely ideas.

My tribe above all was Associate Reformed Presbyterian, A.R.P.'s—the All Right People, my mother said. In a novel currently underway I say of this tribe of ARP's: "The denomination leaned toward theocracy, yet had such joy in singing the Psalms, and such a generous doctrinal view of God's grace that, like an Alpine floral mat, these colored with surprises the colder heights of Calvinism." Their history exploded backward into receding splits and schisms: Presbyterians vs. Reformed Presbyterians, Convenanters against Seceders, Old against New Lights, Pro and Anti-Burghers—these people assumed from habit that contradiction and opposition were natural states, like having your hands, eyes, and feet in double supply.

I took in paradox with my breakfast pablum. I would reel away toward grammar school, head ringing with ordinary weekday admonitions: "Remember you can't make a silk purse out of a sow's ear, but that's no excuse for not trying." No wonder I ended up a teacher. No wonder I ended a realist, convinced of magic.

Paradox sung on that eerie praising note is how the magic got past Calvinism; occasionally pieces of magic even got past John Calvin himself who—though his maximum tribute at his wife's funeral was "She never interfered with my work"—was nonetheless able to find singing powerful for "moving and inflaming the heart," did stock a regular large monthly supply of various wines, and once defended art against those who said music and poetry had sneaked into human culture through the children of Cain. "The invention of arts," Calvin wrote, "is the gift of God"; he even thought truth could be found and admired in those he called "profane" writers.

Anthropologist Mary Tew Douglas, noting that some religions contain more magic than others, calls magic a particular *style* of religion, depending on the efficacy of symbolic forms. What Douglas means is miracle and sacrament; but in my church, words and The Word were almost sub-sacraments themselves, could work wonders, could transubstantiate any old thing by the side of a red-clay road.

This child was at church more than my children were at television. Faulkner, too, has said he assimilated Christianity unawares; "it has nothing to do with how much of it you might believe or disbelieve—it's just there," he said. It was "just there" for me, too, but I did believe, thanks to the dangerous magic of words. "Day unto day uttereth speech and night unto night sheweth knowledge." The Ten Commandments got burned with God's hot finger into the tablets of stone, whether the Israelites could read or not. "In the beginning was the Word, and the Word was with God and the Word *was* God"—they told me that years before I could meet *logos* in koine Greek and start over. In Judges, a man who could not precisely pronounce, teeth together, "Shibboleth," was slain at the passages of Jordan—hard news for us drawlers. And behind the tower of Babel loomed some lost universal and glorious language; no wonder Catholic James Joyce tried to go under the fence to get into that Tower's backyard again.

And Biblical vows had to be kept; to break your word had consequences. Witness Jonah, who traveled inside a whale instead of aboard ship to Nineveh because he knew God wasn't mean enough to wipe the city out. Or, worse, witness Jephtha and his daughter, the day God *was* mean enough. Even to prefeminists, it was clear women had better protect themselves from men's idle, distant promises to a patriarchial god who hadn't—so far—had the good-sense benefits of a human mother. Some Old Testament women chose to shortcut men's promises directly, as Delilah did by taking the shears to Samson's long hair.

In Scripture, too, naming meant power. The Tetragrammaton was not pronounced, though it was whispered to me as a child that if one could speak aloud the entire Old Testament on one mighty exhaling breath, that would be God's true name—but it would also be like removing the golden screw from the golden navel; the Universe would fall down. Even human names could be taken or changed in a blaze at Damascus or, at Bethel, wrestled for against angels. To this day I hesitate when a telephone voice asks crisply, "May I have your name, please?"

And wasn't it clear in Genesis that the universe was made, not from a big bang in the first three minutes, but as matter's obedient response to an imperative sentence?

Years before I read Darwin, *homo sapiens* seemed clear to me as the creature whose speaking and writing gave him dominion over beasts. His distinctive use of words also provided communication with the Infinite as no mute golden calf could ever do. I had a child's version of Walker Percy's comment, "Even the most mechanistic behaviorist would admit that men write books about chimpanzees and dolphins but that chimpanzees and dolphins do not write books about men."

Even nature, despite my tomboy time in trees, was nature interpreted by one particular book: that dove with the green twig plucked for Noah, those lions drowsing off with mighty purrs while Daniel told them stories.

Biblical narrative bends everything to purpose. Events occur against a backdrop of eternity that may at any moment break through, even to stop Balaam's ass in its tracks. This style of writing subdues descriptive detail since, however magical the words, they are less so than the Hidden God they dance around.

I learned much later, of course, that the verbal style of the King James Bible, thinned down from Latin Vulgate, sieved through Greek Septuagint, long after oral Aramaic—that style was already archaic in 1611, greatly influenced by Tyndale; elevated, repetitive, rhythmic, full of echoing parallels more transferable to Whitman's temperament than to mine.

But what I did absorb was the conviction that the Image of God was actually linguistic, that what we called "soul" could only be made manifest in language seen, said, heard, read, riddled and rhymed, parsed, even scribbled by children, on notebooks, in lemon juice, without any tangible loss of magic. Words were the power inside us. Words also had the power to materialize a hand out of thin air to write the future: *Mene mene Tekel Upharsin.* Words could pull cripples to their feet.

Certainly the Bible fed me richer words than my children learned by "Leaving it to Beaver." Metaphor: vine and branches, shepherd and sheep; the central one of the New Testament, "God is Love." Week after week I could leave dull schoolbooks and ugly milltown playgrounds to enter, on Sundays, a land of milk and honey, where mountains clapped their hands, where rivers and morning stars sang together and where lived—beside those rivers, under those melodious stars—not at all pious people but drunken Noah with, as we whispered, his weenie showing; that trickster Jacob; impetuous Simon Peter dogpaddling his clumsy way to sainthood; the Uriah-Bathsheba-David love triangle and its violence— dozens of characters whom Eric Auerbach finds, in *Mimesis*, more tangled, squabbling, ambiguous, and undignified than Homer's.

Eric Auerbach, as you know, was a lifelong student of Giambattista Vico, who thought platonically in a world already skewed toward Aristotle. Vico would have considered me in my childhood pew and all of us lovers of word-magic consistent with his views on history and language. He believed there were three stages that recurred in cycle, three modes of language suited to each stage, and that individuals mirrored small the larger process.

Early on, Vico thought, forest primitives (and small children) were nearly mute with no conscience, no capacity for reflection, mostly dependent on gestures, mimicry, the use of objects or signs for objects. Writing began at the level of alphabet, then syllable, then grew into oral verse with formulaic sound schemes. By parallel, we can now train a chimpanzee to respond to fewer than a hundred hand signals; in the same time a small child will pick up what Noam Chomsky called an "infinite" number of sentences. Then Vico's tribe cleared fields and could build altars on which a visible thing could be burned on behalf of an Invisible Thing. The tribe (and the older child) grew away from the quick world of the senses, much as Walker Percy likes to show Helen Keller's enormous leap from one word for water right over the chimpanzee into the vast linguistic world beyond. The tribe made metaphor, thing-language, imaginative heroic emblems, poetic and symbolic words. We changed sign into symbol. We could dream. We also became superstitious, could see ghosts, scream with nightmare.

In Vico's Phase II came the cities with streets and horizontal vision. The eternal present spread out into time, acquired verb tense and memory of heroes who spoke in noble, elevating language. Now there is a future, a long future; perhaps there will be forever. Slowly, tribal gods fold into one god; even I, one member of the tribe, can speak to Him and write to Him. Metaphor slides into metonymic language and we turn Lamb into bread, Lamb's blood into wine, poetry to prose, romance to realism. Irony and dialectic develop and by Vico's Stage III—the age he lived and wrote in—language had grown more scientific, factual, and descriptive.

Descartes had come along by Stage III, had separated off the mind but thumbtacked it back to the body through the pineal gland. Reason, analysis, abstraction are now emphasized. The good news is that myth matures into science and philosophy; the bad news is how much duller these sound in a language increasingly staid, self-conscious, unimaginative. Since written systems cover most forms of thought in Stage III, language becomes conventional, institutionalized. Words are no longer the things themselves as in the childlike Stage I Tribe; they are less and less one thing put for another as in Stage II; but words are now said to be objective, and tribal writers may feel out of historical phase, be linguistically ahead or behind the times in which they live. Most tribes now hail from Missouri (urban Missouri) and have to be shown. The common people (Vico said "vulgar") succeed to the world of heroes in a tribe where the child becomes middle-aged and predictable. Though he may still have average intimations of mortality, his REM sleep is poor and, besides, under analysis, he has tamed his average dreams through average understanding.

End of cycle, Vico said; it will spin and start over—a theory that, by skipping eschatology, disturbed his church.

Descartes has now been dead 333 years, Vico a century less, even Eric Auerbach since 1957, and many of Vico's ideas have been discarded, but a few keep springing up, like outcrosses of seeded wildflowers in cultivated gardens. Roman Jakobson says metaphor and metonymy parallel the two principles of magic in Fraser's *Golden Bough*. Metaphor's magical ancient sister is Similarity: like produces like; put pins in a voodoo doll; burn Ho Chi Minh in effigy. And Metonym's magic sister is Contagion: the belief that things once close together continue to act on each other, so you must seek the nail clippings of your enemy, must touch the Cross, must allow shed baby teeth to be carried away only by a *good* fairy.

Every metaphor, Vico said, is a short myth. It serves the gods because only the concrete can represent the ineffable, and "tabernacle among us," mystery and magic brought down to earth. In metonymy the overlap of metaphor begins to slide and separate word from thing; literature can even scatter unity until, at extremes, it narrates the contingent and the random. To Freud, the sister of metonymy is displacement wit. Jung's synchronicity, called by some seriality, partakes of it. In *Illness as Metaphor*, some of our deep dread of cancer, so Norman Mailer and Susan Sontag say, comes (even today, in Vico's third and most scientific middle-aged Age) from the magical and metaphoric power leaking into the word *cancer* from behind, just as, last century, we slowed down medical research while we verbally empowered, romanticized, and worsened tuberculosis and gave to Virginia and Edgar Allan Poe the experience their hearts required.

Word-magic functions in this Age for writers and readers from every tribe. Even when print makes and arranges words for the eye, incantation, onomatopoeia and sound still use the mouth and ear. "Mr. Bloom ate with relish the inner organs of beasts and fowls" was written for the salivary gland. And, as William Gass says, "You have to perform Beckett in the mouth." Agreed-on metonymy has also given our age the categorizing we get from word-association tests, vulgarized now on morning television where merchandise is awarded for commonplace thinking. What a change from the days when an accused witch in the river would sink or float! Now atypical language is diagnostic!

Yeats said, "As I altered my syntax, I altered my intellect." In our Age, certain professions not only alter syntax, but shift language into the jargon and euphemism Orwell detested, find ways to say "Watergate was entered" and, by passive voice, make burglars vanish into thin air. People may also regress into Vico's mute stage. Some paralyze an arm rather than speak guilt aloud, leave blanks on a page (Sterne, Oates), film pictures of silence and stillness (Bogart's face, Jack Benny's stare, Chaplin's pause). Some authors can make absence an actual plot experience, as when the boy Walt disappears from the pages after the car crash in *The World According to Garp*.

Language also has the power to call up the invisible, not only the Witch of Endor for Saul or the ghost of Hamlet's father onstage, but routinely, through those ideas whose reality exists in words alone: Freud's vision of the layers of the mind, Heaven, Hell, the statement "I love you" that sometimes causes two people to marry. We discard some language (the four humors) and enlarge some (the four elements). Progress kills off language the way in this century the electron microscope replaced images with literal facts, thus ending certain metaphors; and, oh Democritus, real atoms at last have been really smashed! This black magic we were not ready for.

I break off examples because of the obvious multitude of word-magics, tribes, and writers affected by them in different ways, including us at this symposium wearing traditional feathers and private masks, some postmodern, others in returning cycle to the child's delight in language (hey nonny! and slithy toves) and some of us great clumsy realists, like mastodons.

But unlike the critics' tribe, writers accept, may even wistfully enjoy, their opposites and adversaries, especially writers reared by the ARP's. How I would have liked my prose style to be *in* style, better yet, ahead of it since Pound is right: what the expert is tired of today the public will tire of tomorrow. I would have liked to make crank narrators, to be skillful at cubist collage, to lay down a reflective layer of language that would strike off light like silver plating, to invoke characters as Olympian and feverish as those of D. H. Lawrence (said by some to have been on speed before there even *was* any), to slice a thin found-art found-out life in *City Life*. But Joyce Carol Oates observed that if Wallace Stevens could have written as powerfully as Whitman, no doubt he would have, "but he could not, so his aesthetic theories differ." In style, as Wright Morris says, the original part, if any, lies beyond what we would like or can control.

I cannot transfer late and be at home in the tribe that knows literature as semantics, sees the Sistine Chapel as paint, hears Beethoven's Ninth as sound vibrations, and loves a lover as an appealing cellular mass; but, since all these statements are *true,* I can appreciate literature that from similar premises achieves particular styles. Indeed, I prefer to read those authors different from me; they never reinforce my weaknesses. (I already find writing an abstract art, even in realistic mode. The words *I cried* are very far from the experience of crying. The magic is in how much recollection of actual grief they nonetheless can summon.)

To read and perceive at the level of semantics and paint and cells does not mean I can write there. Inevitably, these must seem half-truths to one reared by the savage Bible Belt tribes, where the "good news" of

God's death was badly reported, slow to arrive, then mostly laid aside as a less useful gospel than the one we were already living by.

This tribal history does not mean that I, a believer, write stories as direct mail, to sign up Miss Boxholder or Mr. Resident into my own tribe. I am not selling God wrapped in my plain brown stories. Nor will it ever be quite my style to exhort through characters, as Will Barrett exhorts, in *The Second Coming*: "Where is it? What is missing? Where did it go? I won't have it! I won't have it! Why this sadness here? Don't stand for it! Get up! Leave! Go live in a cave until you've found the thief who is robbing you. But at least protest. Stop thief! What is missing? God? Find him!"

Percy is surely in my tribe—low country, high church division—but I cannot narrate through Will Barrett, or even Binx Bolling. I'd rather be cast as Ellen, the nurse Dr. Thomas More marries at the end of *Love in the Ruins,* described as a "noble, surprisingly heavy, Presbyterian armful."

Most current literature, even that written by believers, is less bluntly theological than Walker Percy's or Flannery O'Connor's, but even the comics in my tribe at least hope to write prose the way T. S. Eliot wanted to read poems, as "not merely an experience, but a serious experience."

Must such seriousness drive Percy and me and Graham Greene and O'Connor and James Agee and others to war with neighboring tribes whose play with magical words reveals nothing better or worse than delight? Must we oppose those poems that don't mean but *are,* those novels that say life is a fiction (this usage always sounds as if fiction is spelled with a Ph), those plays in which dialogue is reduced to chatter because chatter's the point?

No, we can read and admire work in which the element of artifice becomes a major power.

However, lest you conclude my tribe is all-benevolent, free of self-righteousness and pride, let me add that one of its more pious members is sure to read badly the work from other tribes, look up, and say, mealy-mouthed, that artifice may be a modern form of idolatry; that Nebuchadnezzar, too, commanded Daniel that golden statues deserved worship; that John Calvin was unwilling to find truth in the work of profane writers. I *am* sorry. Believers are sometimes as irascible and unjust as New York critics.

And the Bible *is* heady stuff. Mention Nebuchadnezzar and the allusion nowadays cannot help breaking like a moralizing thunderbolt above Vico's Stage III audiences.

Occasionally, though, such thunder rings loudest in the inner ear, as it did over Gardner's *On Moral Fiction,* whose approach was secular, aesthetic, intellectual, and not didactic, much less Christian. Gardner called John Irving a moral writer, though *The World According to Garp* may not be on the list for the Baptist Ladies League this month. (It's too bad if it is not, as the ladies might ponder why Garp's world is only half post-Christian. It omits religious ritual for terminal cases, and the Father of Lights seems certainly gone from Garp's world; but the Prince of Darkness survives, has been turned back into a frog, an Undertoad, and possesses there, depersonalized, more cold-blooded power than he has been assigned since Milton).

Probably Gardner regretted his arrogant tone in *On Moral Fiction;* he certainly dismissed too easily too many good writers in other good tribes besides his native one. At his best, he only advocated what Morris has called the "head-clearing carbolic whiff of truth." To Gardner, "moral" meant life-giving. Unlike me, he could tell an interviewer, "Fiction is the only religion I have." And we would both oppose what he called that type of literature which would "make hope contingent on acceptance of some religious theory."

But in addition to the pious cousins, my tribe has slow wits, remittance men, hustlers, a few snake-oil salesmen; there will always be some writers there who *do* make hope contingent. Others, like Miguel de Unamuno, get on the Index and stay there. Typically, I get called Gothic, southern, even a feminist writer, not a Christian one; and I'm just as glad. That's a good noun, *Christian,* but it spoils to a rancid adjective. Soon after Christian novelists, you begin to get Christian politicians; then it's not far down to the Christian used-car dealers—hold onto your wallets.

We who do not sell used cars *or* God share Percy's reaction when a woman asked him when he was going to write a really *good* novel, like *The Cardinal.* Artists in any tribe don't see life as a problem to be solved, with hope contingent on narrow doctrine, the women's movement, or even semiotics, though Dorothy L. Sayers, for whom art and faith were so plaited she could find the Trinity embedded in London pavement, identified heresies in literature. All technique and no vision, for instance, was to her like Arianism; the Manichees became propaganda writers promoting the Idea at the expense of the living story in which it should dwell; and a bodiless Gnosticism produced that elegant literary dialogue which no living author could get his tongue around. Sayers is in another division of the tribe—old Empire, Inkling subtype—and she must have invented Lord Peter Wimsey to give herself some rest from that larger Lordship.

Despite tribal affiliations, I have never found life, faith or art nearly so neat. Not all stones have sermons in them. Some of us are relieved. And I continue to outlive many days surveying this world with the suspicion that Deus has really absconded. With the funds.

Since I struggle to believe, I cannot write to Vico's Stage III audience as Flannery O'Connor did, to get its attention by huge startling pictures and shouts. We mothers, kindergarten teachers, and periodic doubters solicit attention by whispering.

If subgroups of my tribe are not identical in volume, style of thought, subject matter, are they and their opposites identifiable by their prose-style ways of telling?

Most college freshman rhetorics (see *The Plain Style* by Hogan and Bogart) categorize five basic tribal styles:

1. The semiliterate style, ranging from the Sacco-Vanzetti letters to deliberate exploitation in *Huckleberry Finn*;
2. The flat style, as in Lloyd Douglas, Zane Grey, some of Hemingway;
3. The ornate style—political speeches, William Faulkner;
4. Experimental style—Stein, Joyce, and inheritors;
5. And the plain style, which the *Hudson Review* has assigned to me.

Most writers, however, make only two main divisions: plain style or fancy. Annie Dillard lists William Gass as fancy, a performance artist who draws attention to fiction's linguistic texture; John Gardner agrees, calling him "the best of the lot." Two divisions of styles are also made in Auerbach's famous chapter, "Odysseus' Scar," where he contrasts Greek with Hebraic styles. Homer, he says, externalizes experience, illuminates and reveals by detail, verisimilitude, and foreground. By contrast, the narrative of Abraham unfolds by subordinating detail to a suspenseful line, while always God smolders out of sight. Auerbach says that, unlike Zeus, only suggestions of the Hebrew God ever materialize. "He always extends into depths." Hebraic narrative relies less on episode than what Daphne Athas calls "the power of the correlative conjunction," where events go on and on without mundane cause, since God is the real protagonist. Faulkner picked up that conjunction trick.

Do today's plain and fancy prose styles divide between Athens/Jerusalem? The aesthetic writers vs. the message writers, even when the messengers whisper? Are the mimetics who render this world plus theme *plain* stylists; are those making worlds from language inevitably fancy?

Could we line up our fiction writers in two rows, for instance, behind the following two quotations?

1. Leslie Fiedler: "Literature is what you remember when you've forgotten all the words"; or
2. William Gass, to the *Paris Review*: "When I read a traditional novel, I never remember anything except language, the rhythms in the language patterns. . . . I think I forgot the plot of *Middlemarch* hours after I read it but not the impression, the quality of its style."

How convenient if styles of thought or belief paired neatly with styles of prose in two big tribes: we plain Hebraic sheep vs. those priapic and agile goats piping to Pan! On the right, all Mary's little lambs, and on the left the Billy Goats Gruff who, instead of wailing and gnashing their teeth, keep on inventing bridges with multicolored trolls underneath, just for the hell of it.

It will not work.

Test some examples.

Anne Tyler. Realist. Grew up in a Quaker commune in Celo, N.C. In clear direct style she might be said to work steadily with prodigal sons and elder stay-at-home brothers, with domestic Marthas and curious Marys who leave or stay according to their inner lights.

But John Updike? Congregationalist. Usually called a realist, though one with a fancy style. Updike differentiates Olinger from Tarbox as stages in his pilgrim's progress, says that he plotted *Couples* mostly in church (which may have given *his* minister some pause). And hasn't Updike said that novels are not the writing of ideas but "objects with different shapes and textures?"

Try prolific Anthony Burgess, a student of language now at work on an Italian translation of *Finnegans Wake*. He calls his novels "medieval Catholic in their thinking." He has attempted many forms, mixed prose with musical structure, invented Clockwork-Orange language, and opposes, as I do, sectarianizing books, since fiction is "after truth, which is not goodness."

Or picture, just for one ironic minute, the face of Anne Sexton, reading her fan letters from the Jesuits while she worked up to suicide.

Here's Stanley Elkin: "Rhetoric doesn't occur in life; it occurs in fiction. . . . a book doesn't have to sell people anything but language. Style yes; lifestyle no." He likes characters to be heroically extravagant. The muse he believes in is serendipity.

It would be hard to lead writers, two-by-two, into some arbitrary ark, our plain and fancy examples. And impossible to get the line to march neatly in pairs past that ominous engraving of Tolstoy, granddaddy of realism, which confronts the reader of Barthelme's "At the Tolstoy Museum." People would fall out of line to split hairs and argue. (Some writers, not all of them sexist, do say that—given heroines and trains—they'd rather read less of Erica Jong's or Mary McCarthy's women *in* them in favor of Anna Karenina, underneath.) One Tolstoy admirer, Ernest Gaines, who structures his fictions with care in muted, understated, even Hebraic prose, shaped one novel in the pattern of Christ's Passover Week. Many other writers, but not all, who seem chiefly committed to theme (religious, historical, sociological) do turn out to be semirealists who put their verbal gifts at theme's service by writing in a modest and low-key style as clear as water, through which their themes can pass.

But, oh! The exceptions! Even my tribe, influenced by Scripture, could choose among sixty-six books; *Job* is in there, *Psalms,* the existential *Ecclesiastes,* the *Song of Songs.* Bare narratives of Ruth and David or parables by Luke may have instructed us short-story writers and taker-outers; but surely James Agee preferred the late rhapsodic chapters of Isaiah.

And what about Carl Sagan preaching the miracles of science in the cosmos on public television once a week? He sounds like Jeremiah, after the prophet took Happiness Lessons.

Margaret Drabble is as fatalistic as the Greeks; Nadine Gordimer believes in the limited goals of Camus—does this show in their prose styles? Saul Bellow counts "not on perfect understanding, which is Cartesian, but on approximate understanding, which is Jewish." The style of his fiction partakes of the essay. And Joan Didion, after citing her harsh

Protestant Ethic and preference for dark journey over the golden mean, then adds that the two types of sentences she most admires are these: Ernest Hemingway's. And Henry James's.

Make your own lists to test style against philosophical content, from C. S. Lewis's *Till We Have Faces* to Mary Renault, from Marge Piercy (Updike says her characters talk like press handouts) to Jerry Bumpus. Compare Larry McMurtry, who says that in the late '70s he lost his Minor Regional Novelist T-shirt in a Texas laundromat, to Alan Paton; compare McMurtry and Paton to Richard Brautigan, now forty-eight and living in Montana;[1] consider Frederick Buechner, a Presbyterian preacher with a highly poetic, fancy style, and Peter de Vries, who has declined requests to lecture on theology at Princeton; Richard Yates, said to dislike postrealist fiction; Tillie Olsen, who bluntly admits that "Tell Me a Riddle" was written to rededicate, to encourage; Gilbert Sorrentino, interested in surface flashes, in language that makes a perfect beauty out of all "the rubbish in the world and in the mind," and William Styron, still using the first-person pronoun in the real, historical world, and still selling books. Look at Vonnegut's individuals in this mechanistic universe, in books containing steadily less and less plot and narration.

No. Patterns won't hold. Minds are neither airtight nor watertight nor changeproof, and members of all tribes have their distinctive fingerprints. I think of William Gaddis's *Recognitions,* and *J.R.*; of Max Apple writing his dissertation on Burton's *Anatomy of Melancholy* while visions of disembodied Castros interrupted; of George Higgins' economical style that talks out loud with no imagery at all; of Reynolds Price, to whom most events occur offstage and get retold by a Greek chorus, in Warren County accent, with Southern Protestant tendencies. Alison Lurie's lucidity is dispassionate, almost snappish. There's Lee Smith's true ear for the pithy speech of both early Appalachia and smalltown pop culture. In her pure style, Eudora Welty wishes to part "the veil of indifference to each other's presence." William Gass, who did his dissertation on metaphor, created Jethro Turbo, preacher; and *Willie Master's Lonesome Wife,* Baby, is certainly having a serious experience, a sexual one. And kiteflyer George Garrett, who finds historical fiction a chance to show the human imagination in action, adds that since we American

1. Since this was written, Richard Brautigan has died.

writers are the tax losses of free enterprise, we may as well write as we please.

This part-time Calvinist might whisper, "Or write as we must."

My trouble is: I've always admired anything magical that any other writer could do. Those extreme members of the tribe of Art and the tribe of Religion always find this admiration wishy-washy.

The attempt to separate plain from fancy, Hebrew from Greek, committed from wishy-washy, thematic from aesthetic writers, etc., leads me to conclude that all good writers belong to at least two tribes; they cannot always be reached at their first address. No birth certificate guarantees regionalism, nor does background forever lock us inside and throw away the key to synagogue, Parthenon, revival tent, or Linguistics Department. Few writers draw all their social security from the classicists or the romantics, the pre-or-posts. Even realists, modified by these times, are rarely headed home like lemmings to be what John Barth called the "let's-get-back-to-good-old-fashioned-19th-century-story-telling-crew." Good writers produce and enjoy good writing of many kinds. And, as Isaac B. Singer complained, "Who cares about the bad writers? They always find a way to get ahead."

I retain strong membership in my first tribe, where the fingerprint was inked and an early working life drew its own lines in the hand. In parts of my style that old membership always shows, since the ARP's taught not Greek logic but Hebraic psychology. Their Bible cared less about how ark or temple looked than how they were built. God could be immanent in prickly bush and baptizing river, but also transcendent outside the story altogether, sometimes vocal: "As the heavens are high above the earth, so are my ways high above your ways."

Because of how that tribe educated me, whenever I do read widely among those with different aesthetic theories, I must sometimes suspend the ingrained habit of wanting to know right away from prose what the *point* is.

Suspending habits, in fact, occurs in many old stories about tribes and individuals. One individual could set forth from Ur of Chaldees, by faith. Grow up in Nazareth but quit carpentry. Like Paul, could be a dropout from Gamaliel's school for Pharisees. Could float in a basket straight into Pharaoh's family.

Of course, in the Bible, such characters had to believe they were doing *right*. But, from Adam on, don't we *all* think we're doing right? Even in our literary styles?

(Sometimes, to rest with a grin on the bedrock of Original Sin can be downright relaxing.)

There is a second tribe that writers may join if they've learned to keep their own fingerprints and allow others to do the same—to live by paradox; to juggle the real and the imagined, art with religion, word-magic and facts, individual as well as tribe, goodness with truth. This second tribe doesn't care if its members *do* right, only if they write well. It's a motley, nomad, suspect tribe, composed of writers who have come from New England Brahmans, iconoclasts, atheists, slaves and slaveholders, Texas Rangers, and Puritans. *All* of them say they are stylists. *All* of them use words as magic. Members sit late outside tents, drinking and quarreling, arguing style, debating whose fingerprint whorls are more symmetrical or pleasing. Very few pious types get adopted here. One rare drunk may fling another into the campfire now and then, aroused by a crucial verb or a connotation. But daytimes most writers sulk in their tents and keep on writing in separate, lonely, distinctive ways. It's hard to erase anyone's fingerprint by rational augment, even by bullying, and unless hands are held to the fire for quite some time, fingerprints usually grow back.

Wright Morris

Being Conscious

At some point during my lifetime the simple, separate person celebrated by Whitman, esteemed by Horace Greeley, satirized and pilloried by Sinclair Lewis, ceased to be our standard unit of measurement. We have an increase in their number, in their well-being, and there is an enlargement in their awareness, but strange to the point of wonder is the fact that this has resulted in a loss of substance. In terms of dollar value we weigh more, in terms of personal value we weigh less than we used to. We might describe this as a loss, a diminishment of consciousness. Quantitative changes that we can appraise and measure have led to qualitative changes that elude us. We are accountable, impersonally, more than ever, but as numbers rather than faces, and the sum of our numbers is less that of a whole than an aggregate.

I attribute this impression, however accurate or farfetched, not to data analysis, or the research of think tanks, or privately funded investigations, but to my life-long addiction to the reading and writing of fiction. It was the fiction of the matter, not the facts, that made me more highly conscious of the conflicts within me, the complexities around me, and the world itself as a novel lacking an intelligible, authorized text. Who could read it? More to the point, who could and should write it? It was precisely the absence of this fiction in the lives of those who needed it most that has resulted in a world best described as only partially conscious.

In aspiring to be more fully conscious, we conspire to live in less darkness. Is being more fully conscious the first stage of seeing in the dark? Changes of the magnitude I have described, along with tremors that are felt before they are measured, are best registered as "feelings," and palpably shrunken expectations, ponderable losses of consciousness. How do we reconcile these losses, as immaterial as sunshine, with our craving to be among those on whom little is lost?

That master of consciousness, Henry James, by whom we measure our fall from grace, was so ill-prepared for the Great War it might have fallen on the earth from space, like Star Wars. James Joyce, too, in exile in Trieste, found the ear distressingly irrelevant to the creation of the uncreated conscience of his race. So far as we can judge, however, half a century later, the Irish appear to be unaltered, but generations of writers continue to be grateful for an expanded literary conscience. "Welcome, O life, they cry!" and go forth to encounter what seems to be left of it.

Thanks to space travel, we have all seen this planet rising on the moon's bleak horizon, a cloud-veiled and mysterious presence that might well arouse longing in nonterrestrial creatures. As we zoom in closer, breaks in the cloud cover reveal a brown landmass, drained by a river that resembles a great branching tree. One of the smaller branches of this tree can be identified as the Platte River of Nebraska. Three score and ten years ago, a small boy sat there under the porch of a house, spying on whatever might be passing. He sat with his eye at one of the holes between the side slats; his consciousness was imprinted with an elusive time-substance from which he will never recover. Where else could he be but at the dark, pulsing center of the world? All around him it orbited, in widening gyres, and in a moment of transcendent mind expansion he would see it floating in the blackness of space, bizarre, unthinkable, yet as familiar as the clouded, blue-green marbles once weighting his pockets. For a timeless instant it would fill his soul with the winds of space.

This matter of our feelings being at odds with the "facts" is one of the things that identify us as human, and not something else. Those born in a certain time and place—and how manage to be born elsewhere?—will find that cloudy, insubstantial feelings will wreak lifelong havoc with the facts, and that an Irish boy born near Dublin and a Jewish-German girl reared in Oakland, California, will prove to share certain mysterious vibrations with that boy in the Platte Valley of Nebraska.

Once upon a time and a very good time it was there was a moocow coming down along the road and this moocow that was coming down along the road met a nicens little boy named baby tuckoo. . . .

This shared world always appears to be at its morning, and what we hear is the first cock to spread its wings and crow.

For some, the first step in consciousness raising is to go into exile. At the turn of the new century, two unusual, not so simple but separate persons, from Oakland, California, were traveling in Europe. In public they presented a memorable tableau:

Both were dressed in chestnut colored corduroy, wearing sandals after the fashion of Raymond Duncan whose friends they were. Too intelligent to care about ridicule, too sure of themselves to bother about what other people thought, they were rich, and he wanted to paint.

Such a couple would not have been unusual in England, or at the watering spas on the continent, but Gertrude and Leo Stein were birds of a feather from the new world. Subconscious forces were at work in both of them, but in one they were on the verge of eruption.

Slowly and in a way it was not astonishing but slowly I was knowing that I was a genius and it was happening and I did not say anything but I was almost ready to begin something.

As we can tell from this sampling, it has already begun. On her brother's recommendation, she had read Flaubert and applied herself to translating one of his tales, *A Simple Heart*. The seeming artlessness of the master's style, the easy flow of events in a timeless present, the inarticulate nature of the subject—a servant by the name of Félicité—made on the receptive mind of Gertrude Stein a profound and memorable impression.

She had also been straining, at this time, to free herself from the influence of her brother, Leo, and involve herself in the lives of two young women. Such a menage à trois, even in Paris, was a taboo subject, and for a woman with Stein's strongly puritan nature and proudly held middle-class morals, a source of great torment. Her first effort to master the tumult of her emotions took the form of a conventional narration, owing much to Henry James. *Things as They Are,* a remarkably good title, challenged Stein to consider the complexities of her nature, and she does not force the book to a false conclusion. It accepts her predicament as a stalemate. It is thanks to this stalemate that we owe the writing of *Three Lives,* where she transforms an intimately personal dilemma to the impersonal world of fiction, the problems of exposure minimized. The audacity of this achievement, the innovations in voice, language and narrative technique without precedent or prior experiment, result in the first radically innovative prose fiction of the century. The imagination breathes more freely once it has adapted to these new rhythms and repetitions; the common word, the commonplace phrasing, is sufficient to capture the uncommon observation. There is little to suggest the intensity of the conflicting emotions.

In friendship power always has its downward curve. One's strength to manage rises always higher until there comes a time one does not win, and though one may really lose, still from the time victory is not sure one's power slowly ceases to be strong.

Full and frank tribute is paid to the power of Stein's emotions in the portrait of Melanctha, who speaks out for the sensual yet ambiguous side of her passionate character. It is characteristic of Stein that she gives no quarter, and sacrifices Melanctha to the impasse she had herself reached in *Things as They Are,* a work that will not be published.

Years later Stein will speak of her debt to Cézanne, from whom she learned that all the parts of a picture are equal, but her talent lay in her unquestioned assurance that the source of this new conscience was a vernacular language that gave voice to a music previously unheard.

Anna found her place with large, abundant women, for such were always lazy, careless, or helpless, and so the burden of their lives could fall on Anna, and give her just content. Anna's must be always these large helpless women, or be men, for none others could give themselves to be so comfortable and free.

Her two years in Baltimore had given her the needed exposure to the talk of black people, which when added to the ferment of her emotions resulted in these lyrical yet commonplace moments, as if in answer to Whitman's call for a new American language.

Sometimes the thought of how all her world was made, filled the complex, desiring Melanctha with despair. She wondered, often, how she could go on living when she was so blue.

Old and new rhythms of speech are subtly blended to approximate the speech for which words seem lacking. The vagaries, deviations, and artful repetitions accurately capture, even as they create, the stream of emotions below the surface. Here indeed, to the extent that it exists, is the stream-of-consciousness that will soon be in fashion. Womanly feeling is paramount, and from the feeling flows the relevant impressions. *The Good Anna,* the *Gentle Lena,* and the ceaselessly tormented *Melanctha* are possessed and revealed in a manner we feel only a woman might have achieved. The world of fiction is peopled by women shaped by the male imagination, but Gertrude Stein might be the first to free herself from the prior, man-fashioned examples. In this remarkable achievement the bottomless depths of her own ego provided the necessary ballast. With apparent ease, as if she needed to be more than conscious, her vernacular reveals lives and emotions not previously the subject of literature.

But she is just beginning. On completing *Three Lives* she turned to a project more in scale to her ample nature. Hints of this History of a Family's Progress had appeared earlier—the word *History* greatly appealed to her love of facts, of the thing itself, of the scrutiny that was possible (so she believed at the time) to the scientist. Dissatisfied with the disarray that presented itself as fiction, at one point she thought of *Three Lives* as a history. She wanted to stress, in *The Making of Americans,* that what she had in mind was no more and never less than the history of an American family's progress.

Fifteen years before Hemingway arrived in Paris she had completed this MS, a work that proved to be longer than Joyce's *Ulysses*. It was given to Hemingway to read, and made on him a celebrated impression. If it was not the best book he had ever read, or tried to, it was certainly one of the strangest, and had on him a predictably disturbing effect. The anxiety of influence would soon rupture the smooth course of his friendship with the author, although he would be mistaken in his feeling that she would be a threatening competitor. She had already moved on to the sort of writing that resembled nothing whatsoever but itself, leaving to Hemingway some of the minor variations on *The Making of Americans.*

On the first page of *The Making of Americans,* Stein greets the reader with these words: "It has always seemed to me a rare privilege, this, of being an American, a real American, one whose tradition it has taken scarcely sixty years to relate. We need only realize our parents, remember our grandparents and know ourselves and our history is complete.

Much that is obsessive and recurrent in American life and literature is clarified in this passage. Little wonder that we are eager to repossess the past. In doing so we hope to recover nothing less than our entire history.

In her accounting, however, this short history will prove to be a long one, and not so easily shared.

We, living now, are always to ourselves young men and women. When we, living always in such feeling, think back to them who make for us a beginning, it is always as grown and old men and women or as little children that we feel them, those whose lives we have just been thinking.

There is a lingering of the music of *Three Lives* in these lines, but she is more insistent as to what she is telling, and how she tells it, and less concerned with charming the reader.

Middle class, middle class, I know no one of my friends who will admit it, one can find no one among you all to belong to it. . . . and yet I am strong, and I am right, and I know it, and I say it to you and you are to listen to it, yes here in the heart of people (Paris) who despise it.

Has the middle class American ever spoken, or heard spoken, such an affirmation of the middle-class life that he has fled the country to be free of, at once puritan and stridently moral. "And I say it to you and you are to listen to it—"

But, of course, no one is listening. The great and ample lady, so assured in her conscience, so proud of her class, spread wide in her chair off the rue de Fleurus, is talking, like most conscious Americans, to herself. In affirmation and assurance her democratic vista is as wide and as deep as Whitman's, and there is no doubt in my mind as to who would be sitting at whose feet during this lecture.

As she talks to us it is clear that her concept of consciousness is repetition: ceaseless repetition, with murmuring variations, inexhaustibly self-generating and self-modifying. She has brooded deeply on the depths of these soundings and is captivated by what she feels. She cannot ponder long and long enough. She cannot repeat what she feels often enough. "Everyone then has a history in them by the repeating of what comes out of them."

The making of Americans is summarized in this statement, and if it stood alone it would have many readers. But hundreds of pages, and hundreds of thousands of words, are devoted to nuances of these sensations in which the willing but weary reader finally loses interest.

I could go on and on, I am so certain that it would be a very important thing. . . . I am so certain that I am knowing a very great deal about being in men and women that it certainly does seem as if something would be missing if not anyone would be coming to know from me all of that everything.

In so far as it seems likely, or desirable, this conscious remaking of Americans approximates "the stream of consciousness" that Joyce, the word magician, will cunningly turn to the triumph of Molly Bloom's soliloquy, and in the fullness of time to *Finnegans Wake.* In these contrasting examples, a supremely conscious artifice, and a supremely conscious intuition combine to innovate a luminous and matchless period in the craft of fiction. This latter we might call *Gerty's Wake,* to which the keys are not given, but the river run is still from swerve of shore to bend of bay and, rather than past Eve, is through her, bringing us at long last back to where we are seated at her feet, nodding in agreement.

Everyone then is an individual being. Everyone is like many others always living, there are many ways of thinking of everyone, this is now a description of all of them. There must then now be a description of all repeating. Now I will tell all the meaning to me in repeating, the loving there is in repeating.

What a great pity it is that the good decent middle class finds it unreadable.

Not long ago the reading of literature led very few people to try to write it. For one thing, it was considered eccentric behavior. Respectable people thought it unrespectable. But both the times and the literature were changing. A crisis of conscience among the more fully conscious, usually brought on and enflamed by the reading of poetry and fiction, persuaded and compelled more and more readers to become writers. Writing, indeed, had become one of a reader's options. In the absence of a supporting social fabric of customs, beliefs and shared experience, the young and more fully conscious among us turned to writing as a form of survival, a means of salvation. Few of them knew it, but the first half of the twentieth century had found many remarkable talents turning to writing as an act of faith, with the novel the revelation of the true gospel. Joyce, Conrad, D. H. Lawrence, T. S. Eliot, Stein, and Virginia Woolf—to cite a sampling of the converts—provided the texts of the new scripture. Critical and scholarly apparatus was soon called for, and supplied, to clarify and supplement the canon. I myself once held in my hands one of the blue-jacketed copies of *Ulysses,* unabridged and illegal, and I still flush with the fervor of that occasion. *Anna Livia Plurabelle,* mint new in its wrapper, brought me the ultimate revelation once it had been decoded. Faith I did not lack, but I wanted preparation. I never questioned where to look, or that I would fail to find it. I knew in my soul the holy writ had been writ, and in the fullness of time I would learn to read it. Mr. Eliot—a prophet with his eye on the past—provided a text with his own crib. Meeting the more crucial test of the true believer, I never lost the conviction that the book I *hadn't* read, the book I still pursued, would prove to be the clue to all that had escaped me.

It is now forgotten that with the publication of *Finnegans Wake,* the more advanced writers and critics felt that the craft of fiction had achieved a summit that made further fiction writing unnecessary. To Joyce's closing words, *End here,* they pronounced a solemn Amen. Joyce provided the cult of writing with its most priestly figure—Stein would bask in this eminence later—an authorized object of veneration for the pilgrims who made it to Paris. One of these admirers, a young man from St. Paul, author of a novel entitled *The Great Gatsby,* on meeting Joyce in Sylvia Beach's bookshop, was so agitated and inspired he offered to leap from the window in tribute. While living in Paris, I felt, with other writers of the time, emotions for Joyce and his work that are usually reserved for faith. Neither the writer nor his work now share this high eminence, but the *act* of writing, among those who are called to it, is more widely accepted than ever as a source of liberation, and life enhancement.

While in exile, in Trieste, Joyce experienced a palpable expansion of both his consciousness and his craft. For one of his pupils, Amalia Popper, he felt and cultivated an attachment that Richard Ellman, his biographer, describes as a "series of slender occurrences and swollen emotions." They had the effect of bringing his erotic and his literary sensations to an unexampled focus. *Giacomo Joyce* is a manuscript of eight pages, written on both sides, which features breaks or pauses in the text that are plainly part of the narrative's texture. These moments of spaced, visible silence alternate with hushed or laconic clusters of words. To speak at all—in the thrall of his emotions—has brought Joyce to a crisis of technique inextricably commingled with his impressions. It is here we find, in essence, the distillate ingredients of his talent.

A ricefield near Vercelli under creamy summer haze. The wings of her drooping hat shadow her false smile. Shadows streak her falsely smiling face, smitten by the hot, creamy light, grey wheyhued shadows under the jawbones, streaks of eggyolk yellow on the moistened brow, rancid yellow humour lurking within the softened pulp of the eyes.

Much might be written, and all of it substantial, on that brief paragraph. Joyce would hold these fragments in reserve for later appropriation in *Ulysses,* and we sense that the language anticipates the intense introspection of Molly, Bloom, and Stephen. These specimens go further in the way they reveal the writer's capacity to concentrate. Indeed, the power to concentrate his faculties, as an artist, and to hold them for these moments of burning focus, may be what is unexampled in Joyce's talent. We are all capable of moments of intense but flickering perception, like the stir of air from a bat's wing, but Joyce could hold his moment in suspension under the glass of his examination.

In my mind's eye—as I reflect on what I have written—I see Joyce in the portrait of Man Ray, one hand to his forehead, his one good eye focused on the page before him, the other covered with the black eye patch. I am persuaded that his diminished sight increased the burning focus of his concentration, a faculty that would prove to be rarer than his remarkable talent.

She raises her arms in an effort to hook at the neck a gown of black veiling. She cannot: no she cannot. She moves backward toward me mutely. I raise my arms to help her: her arms fall. I hold the web soft edges of her gown and drawing them out to hook them I see through the opening of the black veil her lithe body sheathed in an orange shift. It slips its ribbons of moorings at her shoulders and falls slowly: a lithe smooth naked body shimmering with silvery scales. It slips slowly over the slender buttocks of smooth polished silver and over their furrow, a tarnished silver shadow. . . .

This lover would swoon, as well might the reader, if not supported by the writer's detachment. This eye, this voice, and this matchless comingling of concentration and disinterest, are preparing Joyce for the streets of Dublin, where, having spent itself on ornament and restoration, it will come out on the bridge over the Liffey where the particular dissolves in the universal.

A way a lone a last a love a long the riverrun, past Eve and Adam's, from swerve of shore to bend of bay, brings us by commodius vicus of recirculation back to Howth Castle and Environs.

Why did he do this to us right at the moment we were beginning to get the hang of it? Why, indeed, if not for that reason?

The burden of Joyce's achievement—and that was how it was felt by his contemporaries—was draped, in the manner of a shroud, about the shoulders of another Irishman who appeared in Paris in the early thirties. Since the conscience of the race had been created by Joyce, a more modest enterprise was left to Samuel Beckett—the puzzling out of his own aborted beginnings. Quite literally, with figurative connotations, Beckett believed he had not been properly born; that part of him was still cunningly trapped in the womb.

At this time—he was thirty years of age—Beckett's psychic anguish was such that he avoided sleep to spare himself the terror of his nightmares. Physically and mentally tormented, he spent most of his time in bed. At a lecture given in Paris by Carl Jung, he heard mention of a ten-year-old girl whose dreams signified an uncanny premonition of death. She soon died as she had predicted, and Jung made the comment that "she had never been born entirely."

These words were a revelation to Beckett, since they expressed with uncanny accuracy his feelings about himself. It seemed logical to him that if he did, indeed, remember his birth as "painful," this flawed beginning would surely account for and explain the incomplete development of his personality. It is a fact that from this point on his acute symptoms diminish, and he is able to return to his writing.

Beckett was part of the intimate Joyce circle, the first to translate *Anna Livia Plurabelle* into French, but when the two Irishmen were together what they shared the most was silence. E. M. Forster's admonition, "Only connect," falls in the void that lies between these two masters of language with a minor interest in communication, two cocoons that touched and veered away from each other. Beckett's reason for writing in French, rather than in English, was that, in his opinion, English words do too much of the work he would reserve for himself. Another reason would be that in French he was not writing in the language of Joyce and would suffer less the anxiety of influence. If that seems unlikely, with his talent for suffering, write in French was what he actually did, perhaps hoping in this way to free himself from the ties to words that Joyce had cultivated. But there is more than French between Beckett's intent and his practice. Translated back into English, with the author's assistance, the music is even more persuasive.

I shall not be alone, in the beginning. I am of course alone. Alone. That is soon said. Things have to be soon said. And how can one be sure in such darkness? I shall have company. In the beginning. A few puppets. Then I'll scatter them to the winds, if I can. And things, what is the correct attitude toward things? A, to begin with, are they necessary? What a question. But I have few illusions. Things are to be expected. If a thing turns up, for one reason or another, take it into consideration. Where there are people, it is said, there are things.

For a man who recalls his birth as painful, and continues to suffer from it, this is very straightforward and remarkably transparent. One thing it is not is out of this world. It is in this world to the point of madness. No, not madness. How easy it is, reading Beckett, to think and feel like Beckett. To accept the world according to Beckett.

Until the day when your endurance gone, in this world for you without arms, you catch up in your arms the first mangy cur you meet, carry it the time needed for it to love you and you it, then throw it away. Perhaps he had come to that in spite of appearances. Let me try and explain. From things about to disappear I turn away in time. To watch them out of sight, no, I can't do it.

Is there a better way of putting it? A poet tells us "One has only learnt to get the better of words/ For the thing one no longer has to say, or the way in which/ One is no longer disposed to say it."

In the closing lines of *The Unnamable,* there is a sentence that runs for some seven or eight pages.

—you talk of murmurs, distant cries, as long as you can talk, you talk of them before and you talk of them after, more lies, it will be the silence, the one that doesn't last, spent listening, spent waiting, for it to be broken . . . I don't know, that's all words, never wake, all words, there's nothing else, you must go on, that's all I know, they're going to stop, I can feel it, they're going to abandon me, it will be the silence, for a moment, a good few moments, or it will be mine, the lasting one, that didn't last, that still lasts, it will be I, you must go on, I can't go on, you must go on, I'll go on. . . .

One thing to note. The words of Joyce spring from his cunning, his exile, his genius: the words of Beckett spring from his bloody afterbirth. His is such a special case that he might still be curled up in the fetal position, in his room in Paris, waiting and waiting not for Godot, but by his own admission, for a proper birth.

Beckett and Joyce share lives with one compulsive factor: what we might call the statute of option limitations. Joyce makes his way from Dublin to Trieste to Paris—Beckett from Dublin to Paris. These umbilical chords are stretched, twanged, but never broken. In the case of Joyce, the lines of reinforcement far exceed the lines of nurture. He doubles and triples on his losses. The narrow line that is walked wherever these men walk it will go far to explain how quickly and profoundly the gaze of both men turns inward. Stein, too, had been quick to understand that Paris is indispensable to those who accept the world but do their living in exile.

Where "life" touched Joyce, as it did on increasingly painful occasions, the contact was absorbed into his work in progress or suffered as a burden of guilt. He understood his mania, but he was powerless to break its spell. "Since I began Work in Progress," he said in 1922, "I haven't really lived a normal life." Did he mean to imply that he accepted his unexampled monomania as normal? "My book has been a greater reality for me than reality. Everything gives way to it." How strange it seems for *him* to say so! In Joyce the conscience of the artist, the creator, superseded all others. Some years previously a French writer had said, "As for living, let our servants do it for us," and the art-intoxicated writer shared a similar infatuation.

At the moment that Joyce, as a matter of conscience, is compelled to choose between art and life, and chooses art—just then a young writer from Nottingham, in England, has made a contrary decision. It is LIFE in bold capital letters that D. H. Lawrence chooses, but what he says is also a matter of conscience.

Man struggles with his unborn needs and fulfillment. New unfoldings struggle up in torment in him, as buds struggle forth from the midst of a plant. Any man of real individuality tries to know and understand what is happening, even in himself, as he goes along. This struggle for verbal consciousness should not be left out in art. It is a very great part of life. It is not a superimposition of theory. It is the passionate struggle into conscious being.

So there would seem to be, among artists, a matter of conscience, and conscience. In Joyce the uncreated conscience is a matter of words smelted down and reshaped in the smithy of his soul. In Lawrence the words that struggle up in torment in him are the buds of his emerging nature, his newborn life. They are part of his organic ripening and growth. He feels only scorn for the technical audacities and literary revelations of *Ulysses,* unquestioned evidence of the inhibited, frustrated, and prurient nature of the pornographic Irish mind. Lawrence writes:

We are now in a period of crisis. Every man who is acutely alive is acutely wrestling with his own soul. The people who can bring forth the new passion, the new idea, this people will endure. Those others that fix themselves in the old idea, will perish with the new life strangled unborn within them. Men must speak out to one another.

One point they have in common. Both writers are determined to speak out. Both have measurably expanded our own conscious existence. For all of their explicit contradictions—neither would take the time or the trouble to read the other—they share a common passion and are less unique than they believed themselves to be. Sometime before, Walt Whitman had said, "It is time to explain myself—let us stand up."

At the time Samuel Beckett arrived in Paris a remarkable novel had just been published, one of the many that would not be read by Stein or Joyce or Lawrence.

Journey to the End of the Night scandalized public taste, but it was not thought to be much of a consciousness-raiser. A few years later, however, Beckett read it and admitted he thought it a great novel. As we read it, we are hardly surprised by his opinion. Just in passing, Céline observes: "It would be good to know why it is that one is never cured of loneliness." Indeed. "To love is nothing," he says, "it's hanging together that's so hard."

We spare ourselves most of what he said, since we find it pretty depressing reading, but there is a passion for truth in Céline's tormented nature that redeems his self-disgust. "One might as well make no mistake about it, human beings have very little to say to each other."

Nor is it difficult to see the appeal of this writer for Beckett. I continue to wonder if his copy of the novel has the same underlined passages that mine has, one in particular.

There's nothing frightful in us and on earth and perhaps in heaven above except what has not been said. We shall never be at peace until everything has been said, once and for all time: then there will be silence and one will no longer be afraid of being silent. It will be alright [sic] then.

Reading Céline, a writer of Beckett's temperament might have experienced the full cost of consciousness-raising and found it unacceptable. Indeed, he might have regretted he had become one of those on whom so little was lost. Whatever now stalks toward Bethlehem to be born, and the writer of fiction is one of those who is free to wonder, he is increasingly reluctant to join the procession. The craft of consciousness-raising is not lost, and by a few it will always be practiced, but it now appears to have the limited uses we associate with hanggliding and skydiving. In what we might describe as a shared holding operation, the contemporary writer is committed to conscience maintenance and support—to holding time-honored gains and diminishing crucial losses. At the end of Frank O'Connor's story, "Guests of the Nation," the narrator tells us:

It is so strange—what you feel at such moments, and not to be written afterwards. Noble says he felt he had seen everything ten times as big, perceived nothing around him but the little patch of black bog with the two Englishmen stiffening into it; but with me it was the other way, as though the patch of bog where the two Englishmen were was a thousand miles away from me, and even Noble mumbling just behind me and the old woman and the birds, and the bloody stars were all far away, and I was very small and very lonely. And everything that ever happened to me after I never felt the same about again.

To that all writers, in one voice, would say Amen. What we feel at such moments, and proves so hard to write about, is being conscious on a new and unfamiliar level, where anything that ever happens to us afterward we never feel the same about again.

Donald Barthelme

Let us suppose that someone is writing a story. From the world of conventional signs he takes an azalea bush and plants it in a pleasant park. He takes a gold pocket watch from the world of conventional signs and places it under the azalea bush. He takes from the same rich source a handsome thief and a chastity belt, places the thief in the chastity belt and lays him tenderly under the azalea, not neglecting to wind the gold pocket watch so that its ticking will, at length, awaken the now-sleeping thief. From the Sarah Lawrence campus he borrows a pair of seniors, Jacqueline and Jemima, and sets them to walking in the vicinity of the azalea bush and the handsome, chaste thief. Jacqueline and Jemima have just failed the Graduate Record Examination and are cursing God in colorful Sarah Lawrence language. What happens next?

Of course, I haven't the faintest idea.

It's appropriate to pause and say that the writer is a man who, embarking upon a task, does not know what to do. I cannot tell you, at this moment, whether Jacqueline and Jemima will succeed or fail in their effort to jimmy the chastity belt's lock, or whether the thief, whose name is Zeno and who has stolen the answer sheets for the next set of Graduate Record examinations, will pocket the pocket watch or turn it over to the nearest park employee. The fate of the azalea bush, whether it will bloom or strangle in a killing frost, is unknown to me.

Donald Barthelme

A very conscientious writer might purchase an azalea at the Downtown Nursery, a gold watch at Tiffany's, hire a handsome thief fresh from Riker's Island, obtain the loan of a chastity belt from the Metropolitan, inveigle Jacqueline and Jemima in from Bronxville, and arrange them all under glass for study, writing up the results in honest, even fastidious prose. But in doing so he places himself in the realm of journalism or sociology. The not-knowing is crucial to art, is what permits art to be made. Without the scanning process engendered by not-knowing, without the possibility of having the mind move in unanticipated directions, there would be no invention.

This is not to say that I don't know anything about Jacqueline or Jemima, but what I do know comes into being at the instant it's inscribed. Jacqueline, for example, loathes her mother, whereas Jemima dotes on hers—I discover this by writing the sentence that announces it. Zeno was fathered by a—what? Polar bear? Roller skate? Shower of gold? I opt for the shower of gold, for Zeno is a hero (although he's just become one by virtue of his golden parent). Inside the pocket watch there is engraved a legend, can I make it out? I think so: *Drink me,* it says. No, no, can't use it, that's Lewis Carroll's. But could Zeno be a watch-swallower rather than a thief? No again, Zeno'd choke on it, and so would the reader. There are rules.

Writing is a process of dealing with not-knowing, a forcing of what and how. We have all heard novelists testify to the fact that, beginning a new book, they are utterly baffled as to how to proceed, what should be written and how it might be written, even though they've done a dozen. At best there's a slender intuition, not much greater than an itch. The anxiety attached to this situation is not inconsiderable. "Nothing to paint and nothing to paint with," as Beckett says of Bram van Velde. The not-knowing is not simple, because it's hedged about with prohibitions, roads that may not be taken. The more serious the artist, the more problems he takes into account, the more considerations limit his possible initiatives—a point to which I shall return.

What kind of fellow is Zeno? How do I know until he's opened his mouth?

"*Gently, ladies, gently,*" says Zeno, as Jacqueline and Jemima bash away at the belt with a spade borrowed from a friendly park employee. And to the park employee: "Somebody seems to have lost this-here watch."

38

Let us change the scene.

Alphonse, the park employee from the preceding episode, he who lent the spade, is alone in his dismal room on West Street (I could position him as well in a four-story townhouse on East Seventy-second, but you'd object, and rightly so; verisimilitude forbids it, nothing's calculated quicker than a salary). Alphonse, like so many toilers in the great city, is not as simple as he seems. Like those waiters who are really actors and those cab drivers who are really composers of electronic music, Alphonse is sunlighting as Parks Department employee although he is, in reality, a literary critic. We find him writing a letter to his friend Gaston, also a literary critic although masquerading pro tem as a guard at the Whitney Museum. Alphonse poises paws over his Smith-Corona and writes:

Dear Gaston,

Yes, you are absolutely right—Postmodernism is dead. A stunning blow, but not entirely surprising. I am spreading the news as rapidly as possible, so that all of our friends who are in the Postmodernist "bag" can get out of it before their cars are repossessed and the insurance companies tear up their policies. Sad to see Postmodernism go (and so quickly!). I was fond of it. As fond, almost, as I was of its grave and noble predecessor, Modernism. But we cannot dwell in the done-for. The death of a movement is a natural part of life, as was understood so well by the partisans of Naturalism, which is dead.

I remember exactly where I was when I realized that Postmodernism had bought it. I was in my study with a cup of tequila and William Y's new book, *One-Half*. Y's work is, we agree, good—*very* good. But who can make the leap to greatness while dragging after him the burnt-out boxcars of a dead aesthetic? Perhaps we can find new employment for him. On the roads, for example. When the insight overtook me, I started to my feet, knocking over the tequila, and said aloud (although there was no one to hear), "What? Postmodernism, too?" So many, so many. I put Y's book away on a high shelf and turned to the contemplation of the death of Plainsong, 958 A.D.

By the way: Structuralism's tottering. I heard it from Gerald, who is at Johns Hopkins and thus in the thick of things. You don't have to tell everybody. Frequently, idle talk is enough to give a movement that last little "push" that topples it into its grave. I'm convinced that's what happened to the New Criticism. I'm persuaded that it was Gerald, whispering in the corridors.

On the bright side, one thing that is dead that I don't feel too bad about is

Existentialism, which I never thought was anything more than Phenomenology's bathwater anyway. It had a good run, but how peeving it was to hear all those artists going around talking about "the existential moment" and similar claptrap. Luckily, they have stopped doing that now. Similarly, the Nouveau Roman's passing did not disturb me overmuch. "Made dreariness into a religion," you said, quite correctly. I know this was one of your pared-to-the-bone movements and all that, but I didn't even like what they left out. A neat omission usually raises the hairs on the back of my neck. Not here. Robbe-Grillet's only true success, for my money, was with *Jealousy,* which I'm told he wrote in a fit of.

Well, where are we? Surrealism gone, got a little sweet toward the end, you could watch the wine of life turning into Gatorade. Sticky. Altar Poems—those constructed in the shape of an altar for the greater honor and glory of God—have not been seen much lately: missing and presumed dead. The Anti-Novel is dead; I read it in the *Times*. The Anti-Hero and the Anti-Heroine had a thing going which resulted in three Anti-Children, all of them now at Dalton. The Novel of the Soil is dead, as are Expressionism, Impressionism, Futurism, Imagism, Vorticism, Regionalism, Realism, the Kitchen Sink School of Drama, the Theatre of the Absurd, the Theatre of Cruelty, Black Humor, and Gongorism. You know all this; I'm just totting up. To be a Pre-Raphaelite in the present era is to be somewhat out of touch. And, of course, Concrete Poetry—sank like a stone.

So we have a difficulty. What shall we call the New Thing, which I haven't encountered yet but which is bound to be out there somewhere? Post-Postmodernism sounds, to me, a little lumpy. I've been toying with the Revolution of the Word, II, or the New Revolution of the Word, but I'm afraid the Jolas estate may hold a copyright. It should have the word "new" in it somewhere. The New Newness? Or maybe the Post-New? It's a problem. I await your comments and suggestions. If we're going to slap a saddle on this rough beast, we've got to get moving.

> Yours,
> Alphonse

If I am slightly more sanguine than Alphonse about postmodernism, however dubious about the term itself and not altogether clear as to who is supposed to be on the bus and who is not, it's because I locate it in relation to a series of problems, and feel that the problems are durable ones. Problems are a comfort. Wittgenstein said of philosophers that some of them suffer from "loss of problems," a development in which everything seems quite simple to them, and what they write becomes (I'm quoting) "immeasurably shallow and trivial." The same can be said of writers. Before I mention some of the specific difficulties I have in mind, I'd like at least to glance at some of the criticisms that have been leveled at the alleged postmodernists—let's say John Barth, William Gass, John Hawkes, Robert Coover, William Gaddis, Thomas Pynchon, and myself in this country, Calvino in Italy, Peter Handke and Thomas Bernhard in Germany, although many other names could be invoked. The criticisms run roughly as follows: that this kind of writing has turned its back on the world, is in some sense not about the world but about its own processes, that it is masturbatory, certainly chilly, that it excludes readers by design, speaks only to the already tenured, or that it does not speak at all, but instead, like Frost's Secret, sits in the center of a ring and Knows.

I would ardently contest each of these propositions, but it's rather easy to see what gives rise to them. The problems that seem to me to define the writer's task at this moment (to the extent that he has chosen them as his problems) are not of a kind that make for ease of communication, for work that rushes toward the reader with outflung arms— rather, they're the reverse. Let me cite three such difficulties that I take to be important, all having to do with language. First, there is art's own project, since Mallarmé, of restoring freshness to a much-handled language, essentially an effort toward finding a language in which making art is possible at all. This remains a ground theme, as potent, problematically, today as it was a century ago. Second, there is the political and social contamination of language by its use in manipulation of various kinds over time and the effort to find what might be called a "clean" language, problems associated with the Roland Barthes of *Writing Degree Zero* but also discussed by Lukács and others. Finally, there is the pressure on language from contemporary culture in the broadest sense—I mean our devouring commercial culture—which results in a double impoverishment, theft of complexity from the reader, theft of the reader from the writer.

These are by no means the only thorny matters with which the writer has to deal, nor (allowing for the very great differences between the practitioners under discussion) does every writer called postmodern respond to them in the same way and to the same degree, nor is it the case that other writers of quite different tendencies are innocent of these concerns. If I call these matters "thorny" it's because any adequate attempt to deal with them automatically creates barriers to the ready assimilation of the work. Art is not difficult because it wishes to be difficult, rather because it wishes to be art. However much the writer might long to be, in his work, simple, honest, straightforward, these virtues are no longer available to him. He discovers that in being simple, honest, straightforward, nothing much happens: he speaks the speakable, whereas we are looking for the as-yet unspeakable, the as-yet unspoken.

With Mallarmé the effort toward mimesis, the representation of the external world, becomes a much more complex thing than it had been previously. Mallarmé shakes words loose from their attachments and bestows new meanings upon them, meanings that point not toward the external world but toward the Absolute, acts of poetic intuition. This is a fateful step; not for nothing does Barthes call him the Hamlet of literature. It produces, for one thing, a poetry of unprecedented difficulty. You will find no Mallarmé in Bartlett's *Familiar Quotations*. Even so ardent an admirer as Charles Mauron speaks of the sense of alienation enforced by his work. Mauron writes: "All who remember the day when first they looked into the *Poems* or the *Divagations* will testify to that curious feeling of *exclusion* which put them, in the face of a text written with *their* words, (and moreover, as they could somehow feel, magnificently written), suddenly outside their own language, deprived of their rights in a common speech, and, as it were, rejected by their oldest friends." Mallarmé's work is also, and perhaps most importantly, a step toward establishing a new ontological status for the poem, as an object in the world rather than a representation of the world. But the ground seized is dangerous. After Mallarmé the struggle to renew language becomes a given for the writer, his exemplary quest an imperative. Mallarmé's work, "this whisper that is so closer to silence," as Marcel Raymond calls it, is at once a liberation and a loss to silence of a great deal of territory.

The silencing of an existing rhetoric, in Harold Rosenberg's phrase, is also what is at issue in Barthes' deliberations in *Writing Degree Zero* and after—in this case a variety of rhetorics seen as actively pernicious rather than as passively inhibiting. The question is, what is the complicity of language in the massive crimes of fascism, Stalinism, or (by implication) our own policies in Viet Nam? In the control of societies by the powerful and their busy functionaries? If these abominations are all in some sense facilitated by, made possible by, language, to what degree is that language ruinously contaminated? (These considerations were also raised by George Steiner in his well-known essay "The Hollow Miracle" and, much earlier, by George Orwell.) I am sketching here, inadequately, a fairly complex argument; I am not particularly taken with Barthes' tentative solutions but the problems command the greatest respect. Again, we have language deeply supicious of its own behavior; although this suspicion is not different in kind from Hemingway's noticing, early in the century, that words like *honor, glory,* and *country* were perjured, bought, the skepticism is far deeper now, and informed as well by the investigations of linguistic philosophers, structuralists, semioticians. Even conjunctions must be inspected carefully. "I read each word with the feeling appropriate to it," says Wittgenstein. "The word 'but' for example with the but-feeling—" He is not wrong. Isn't the but-feeling, as he calls it, already sending us headlong down a greased slide before we've had the time to contemplate the proposition it's abutting? Quickly now, quickly—when you hear the phrase "our vital interests" do you stop to wonder whether you were invited to the den, Zen, Klan or coven meeting at which these were defined? Did you speak?

To turn to the action of contemporary culture on language, and thus on the writer, the first thing to be noticed is a loss of reference. If I want a world of reference to which all possible readers in this country can respond, there is only one universe of discourse available, that in which the Love Boat on seas of passion like a Flying Dutchman of passion and the dedicated men in white of *General Hospital* pursue, with evenhanded diligence, triple bypasses, and the nursing staff. This limits things somewhat. The earlier newspaper culture, which once dealt in a certain amount of nuance and zestful, highly literate hurly-burly, has deteriorated shockingly. The newspaper I worked for as a raw youth, thirty years ago, is today a pallid imitation of its former self. Where once we could put spurious quotes in the paper and attribute them to Ambrose Bierce and be fairly sure that enough readers would get the joke to make the joke worthwhile, from the point of view of both reader and writer, no such common ground now exists. The situation is not peculiar to this country. George Steiner remarks of the best current journalism in Germany that, read against an average number of the *Frankfurter Zeitung* of pre-Hitler days, it's difficult at times to believe that both are written in German. At the other end of the scale much of the most exquisite description of the world, discourse about the world, is now being carried on in mathematical languages obscure to most people—certainly to me—and the contributions the sciences once made to our common language in the form of coinages, new words and concepts, are now available only to specialists. When one adds the ferocious appropriation of high culture by commercial culture—it takes, by my estimate, about forty-five minutes for any given novelty in art to travel from the Mary Boone Gallery on West Broadway to the display windows of Henri Bendel on Fifty-seventh Street—one begins to appreciate the seductions of silence.

Problems, in part, define the kind of work the writer chooses to do, and are not avoided but embraced. A writer, says Karl Kraus, is a man who can make a riddle out of an answer.

Let me begin.

Jacqueline and Jemima are instructing Zeno, who's returned the purloined GRE documents and is thus restored to dull respectability, in Postmodernism. Postmodernism, they tell him, has turned its back on the world, is not about the world but about its own processes, is masturbatory, certainly chilly, excludes readers by design, speaks only to the already tenured, or does not speak at all, but instead—

Zeno, to demonstrate that he too knows a thing or two, quotes the critic Perry Meisel on semiotics. "Semiotics," he says, "is in a position to claim that no phenomenon has any ontological status outside its place in the particular information system from which it draws its meaning"—he takes a large gulp of his Gibson—"and therefore, all language is finally groundless." I am eavesdropping and I am much reassured. This insight is one I can use. Gaston, the critic who is a guard at the Whitney Museum, is in love with an IRS agent named Madelaine, the very IRS agent, in fact, who is auditing my return for the year 1979. "Madelaine," I say kindly to her over lunch, "semiotics is in a position to claim that no phenomenon has any ontological status outside its place in the particular information system from which it draws its meaning, and therefore, all language is finally groundless, including that of those funny little notices you've been sending me." "Yes," says Madelaine kindly, pulling from her pocket a large gold pocket watch that Alphonse has sold Gaston for twenty dollars, her lovely violet eyes atwitter, "but some information systems are more enforceable than others." Alas, she's right.

If the writer is taken to be the work's way of getting itself written, a sort of lightning rod for an accumulation of atmospheric disturbances, a St. Sebastian absorbing in his tattered breast the arrows of the Zeitgeist, this changes not very much the traditional view of the artist. But it does license a very great deal of critical imperalism.

This is fun for everyone. A couple of years ago I received a letter from a critic requesting permission to reprint a story of mine as an addendum to the piece he had written about it. He attached a copy of my story he proposed to reproduce, and I was amazed to find that my poor story had sprouted a set of tiny numbers—one to eighty-eight, as I recall—an army of tiny numbers marching over the surface of my poor distracted text. Resisting the temptation to tell him that all the tiny numbers were in the wrong places, which occurred to me, I gave him permission to do what he wished, but I did notice that by a species of literary judo the status of my text had been reduced to that of footnote.

There is, in this kind of criticism, an element of aggression that gives one pause. Deconstruction is an enterprise that announces its intentions with startling candor. Any work of art depends upon a complex series of interdependences. If I wrench the rubber tire from the belly of Rauschenberg's famous goat to determine, in the interest of a finer understanding of same, whether the tire is a B. F. Goodrich or a Uniroyal, the work collapses, more or less behind my back. I say this not because I find this kind of study valueless but because the mystery worthy of study, for me, is not the signification of parts but how they come together, the tire wrestled over the goat's hind legs. Calvin Tomkins tells us in *The Bride and the Bachelors* that Rauschenberg himself says that the tire seemed "something as unavoidable as the goat." To see both goat and tire as "unavoidable" choices, in the context of art-making, is to illuminate just how strange the combinatorial process can be. Nor was the choice a hasty one; Tomkins tells us that the goat had been in the studio for three years and had appeared in two previous versions (the final version is entitled "Monogram") before it met the tire.

Contemporary critics speak of "recuperating" a text, suggesting an accelerated and possibly strenuous nursing back to health of a basically sickly text, very likely one that did not even know itself to be ill. I would argue that in the competing methodologies of contemporary criticism, many of them quite rich in implications, a sort of tyranny of great expectations obtains, a rage for final explanations, a refusal to allow a work the mystery that is essential to it. I hope I am not myself engaging in mystification if I say simply that the mystery exists, not that the attempt should not be made to penetrate it. I see no immediate way out of the paradox—tear a mystery to tatters and you have tatters, not mystery—merely note it and pass on.

We can, however, wonder for a moment why the goat girdled with its tire is somehow a magical object rather than, say, only a dumb idea. Harold Rosenberg speaks of the contemporary artwork as "anxious," as wondering: Am I a masterpiece or simply a pile of junk? (If I take many of my examples here from the art world rather than the world of literature, it's because the issues are more quickly seen in terms of the first: "goat" and "tire" are standing in for pages of prose, pounds of poetry.) What precisely is it in the coming together of goat and tire that is magical? It's not the surprise of seeing the goat attired, although that's part of it. One might say, for example, that the tire *contests* the goat, *contradicts* the goat, as a mode of being, even that the tire *reproaches* the goat, in some sense. That on the simplest punning level, the goat is *tired*. Or that the unfortunate tire has *been caught by* the goat, which has been fishing in the Hudson—goats eat anything, as everyone knows—or that the goat is being *consumed by* the tire, it's outside, after all; mechanization takes command. Or that the goateed goat is protesting the fatigue of its friend, the tire, by wearing it as a sort of STRIKE button. Or that two contrasting models of infinity are being presented, tires and goats both being infinitely reproducible, the first depending on the good fortunes of the B. F. Goodrich Company and the second upon the copulatory enthusiasm of goats—parallel production lines suddenly met. And so on. What is magical about the object is that it at once invites and resists interpretation. Its artistic worth is measurable by the degree to which it remains, after interpretation, vital—meaning that no interpretation or cardiopulmonary push-pull can exhaust or empty it.

In what sense is the work "about" the world, the world that Jacqueline and Jemima have earnestly assured Zeno it's turned its scarlet rump to? It is to this vexing question that we shall turn next.

Let us discuss the condition of my desk. It is messy, mildly messy. The messiness is both physical (coffee cups, cigarette ash) and spiritual (unpaid bills, unwritten novels). The emotional life of the man who sits at the desk is also messy: I am in love with a set of twins, Hilda and Heidi, and in a fit of enthusiasm I have joined the Bolivian army. The apartment in which the desk is located seems to have been sublet from Moonbeam

McSwine. In the streets outside the apartment, melting snow has revealed a choice assortment of decaying et cetera. Furthermore, the social organization of the country is untidy; the world situation is in disarray. How do I render all this messiness, and if I succeed, what have I done?

In a commonplace way we agree that I attempt to find verbal equivalents for whatever it is I wish to render. The unpaid bills are easy enough, I need merely quote one: FINAL DISCONNECT NOTICE. Hilda and Heidi are somewhat more difficult. I can say that they are beautiful—why not?—and you will more or less agree, although the bald statement has hardly stirred your senses. I can describe them—Hilda has the map of Bolivia tattooed on her right cheek and Heidi habitually wears, on her left hand, a set of brass knucks wrought of solid silver—and they move a step closer. Best of all, perhaps, I can permit them to speak, for they speak much as we do.

"On Valentine's Day," says Hilda, "he sent me oysters, a dozen and a half."

"He sent me oysters too," says Heidi, "two dozen."

"Mine were long-stemmed oysters," says Hilda, "on a bed of the most wonderful spinach."

"Oh yes, spinach," says Heidi, "he sent me spinach too, miles and miles of spinach, wrote every bit of it himself."

To render "messy" adequately, that is, to the point that you are enabled to feel it—I don't want you to recognize only that it's there, it should, ideally, frighten your shoes—I would have to be more graphic than the decorum of the occasion allows. What should be emphasized is that one proceeds by way of particulars. If I know how a set of brass knuckles feels on Heidi's left hand it's because I bought one once, in a pawnshop, not to smash up someone's face but to exhibit on a pedestal in a museum show devoted to cultural artifacts of ambivalent status. The world enters the work as it enters our ordinary lives, not as a world-view or system but in sharp particularity: a tax notice from Madelaine, a snowball containing a résumé from Gaston.

The words with which I attempt to render "messy," like any other words, are not inert, rather they're furiously busy. We do not mistake the words *the taste of chocolate* for the taste of chocolate itself but neither do we miss the tease in *taste,* the shock in *chocolate.* Words have halos, patinas, overhangs, echoes. The word *halo,* for instance, may invoke St. Hilarius, of whom we've seen too little lately. The word *patina* brings back the fine pewtery shine on the saint's halo. The word *overhang* reminds us that we have, hanging over us, a dinner date with St. Hilarius, that crashing bore. The word *echo* restores to us Echo herself, poised like the White Rock girl on the overhang of a patina of a halo—infirm ground, we don't want the poor spirit to pitch into the pond where Narcissus blooms, eternally; they'll bump foreheads, or maybe other parts closer to the feet, a scandal— There's chocolate smeared all over Hilarius's halo, messy, messy. . . .

The combinatorial agility of words, the exponential generation of meaning once they're allowed to go to bed together, allows the writer to surprise himself, makes art possible, reveals how much of Being we haven't yet encountered. It could be argued that computers can do this sort of thing for us, with critic-computers monitoring their output; they're madly ambitious. When computers learn how to make jokes, artists will be in serious trouble. But artists will respond in such a way as to make art impossible for the computer. They will redefine art to take into account, that is, exclude, technology, photography's impact upon painting and painting's brilliant response being a clear and comparatively recent example.

The prior history of words is one of the aspects of language the world uses to smuggle itself into the work. If words can be contaminated by the world they can also carry with them into the work trace elements of world which can be used in a positive sense. We must allow ourselves the advantages of our disadvantages.

A late bulletin: Hilda and Heidi have had a baby, with which they're thoroughly displeased, it's got no credit cards and can't speak French, they'll send it back. . . . Messy.

Style is not much a matter of choice. One does not sit down to write and say: Is this poem going to be a Queen Anne poem, a Beidermeyer poem, a Vienna Secession poem or a Chinese Chippendale poem? Rather it is both a response to constraint and a seizing of opportunity. Very often a constraint is an opportunity. It would seem impossible to write *Don Quixote* once again, yet Borges has done so with great style, improving on the original, as he is not slow to tell us, while remaining faithful to it, faithful as a tick on a dog's belly. I don't mean that whim does not intrude; it does. Why do I avoid, as much as possible, using the semi-colon? Let me be plain: the semi-colon is ugly, ugly as a tick on a dog's belly. I pinch them out of my prose. The great German writer Arno Schmidt, punctuation-drunk, averages eleven to a page.

Style is of course *how,* and the degree to which *how* has become *what* since, say, Flaubert is a question that men of conscience wax wroth about, and should. If I say of my friend that on this issue his marbles are a little flat on one side, this does not mean that I do not love my friend. He, on the other hand, considers that I am ridden by strange imperatives, and that the little piece I gave to the world last week, while nice enough in its own way, would have been vastly better had not my deplorable aesthetics caused me to score it for banjulele, cross between a banjo and a uke. Bless Babel.

Let us suppose that I am the toughest banjulele player in town and that I have contracted to play "Melancholy Baby" for six hours before an audience that will include the four next-toughest banjulele players in town. We imagine the smoky basement club, the hustling waiters (themselves students of the jazz banjulele), Jacqueline, Jemima, Zeno, Alphonse, Gaston, Madelaine, Hilda and Heidi forming a congenial group at the bar. There is one thing of which you may be sure: I am not going to play "Melancholy Baby" as written. Rather I will play something that is parallel, in some sense, to "Melancholy Baby," based upon the chords of "Melancholy Baby," made out of "Melancholy Baby," having to do with "Melancholy Baby"—commentary, exegesis, elaboration, contradiction. The interest of my construction, if any, is to be located in the space between the new entity I have constructed and the "real" "Melancholy Baby," which remains in the mind as the horizon that bounds my efforts.

This is, I think, the relation of art to the world. I suggest that art is always a meditation upon external reality rather than a representation of external reality. If I perform even reasonably well, no one will accuse me of not providing a true, verifiable, note-for-note reproduction of "Melancholy Baby"—it will be recognized that this was not what I was after. Twenty years ago I was much more convinced of the autonomy of the literary objects than I am now, and even wrote a rather persuasive defense of the proposition that I have just rejected, that the object is itself world. Beguiled by the rhetoric of the time—typified by a quite good magazine called *It Is,* published by the sculptor Phillip Pavia—I felt that the high ground had been claimed and wanted to place my scuffed cowboy boots right there. The proposition's still attractive. What's the right answer? Bless Babel.

A couple of years ago I visited Willem de Kooning's studio in East Hampton, and when the big doors are opened one can't help seeing—

it's a shock—the relation between the rushing green world outside and the paintings. Precisely how de Kooning manages to distill nature into art is a mystery, but the explosive relation is there, I've seen it. Once when I was in Elaine de Kooning's studio on Broadway, at a time when the metal sculptor Herbert Ferber occupied the studio immediately above, there came through the floor a most horrible crashing and banging. "What in the world is that?" I asked, and Elaine said, "Oh, that's Herbert thinking."

Art is a true account of the activity of mind. Because consciousness, in Husserl's formulation, is always consciousness *of* something, art thinks ever of the world, cannot not think of the world, could not turn its back on the world even if it wished to. This does not mean that it's going to be honest as a mailman; it's more likely to appear as a drag queen. The problems I mentioned earlier, as well as others not taken up, enforce complexity. "We do not spend much time in front of a canvas whose intentions are plain," writes Cioran, "music of a specific character, unquestionable contours, exhausts our patience, the over-explicit poem seems . . . incomprehensible." Flannery O'Connor, an artist of the first rank, famously disliked anything that looked funny on the page, and her distaste has widely been taken as a tough-minded put-down of puerile experimentalism. But did she also dislike anything that looked funny on the wall? If so, a severe deprivation. Art cannot remain in one place, a certain amount of movement, up, down, across, even a gallop toward the past, is a necessary precondition.

Style enables us to speak, to imagine again. Beckett speaks of "the long sonata of the dead"—where on earth did the word *sonata* come from, imposing as it does an orderly, even exalted design upon the most disorderly, distressing phenomenon known to us? The fact is not challenged, but understood, momentarily, in a new way. It's our good fortune to be able to imagine alternative realities, other possibilities. We can quarrel with the world, constructively (no one alive has quarrelled with the world more extensively or splendidly than Beckett). "Belief in progress," says Baudelaire, "is a doctrine of idlers and Belgians." Perhaps. But if I have anything unorthodox to say, it's that I think art's project is fundamentally meliorative. The aim of meditating about the world is finally to change the world. It is this meliorative aspect of literature that provides its ethical dimension. We are all Upton Sinclairs, even that Hamlet, Stephane Mallarmé.

Max Apple

The Style of Middle Age

Literature misses out on most of the fun of art. We don't get colors or new materials or music, just a lot of "he saids" and "she saids" mingled with greed and passion and ambition and bounded by the death of the characters or the laziness of the author or both.

I would illustrate these pages, if I could, with slides, partly to correct this sensory defect of literature. But the figures I want are not available in the configurations I need. So, dear reader, I ask you to bear with me for what we used to call "word pictures." Since they are only words and since I am such a clumsy painter even in words, I ask you to help by daydreaming a little. Please add the color and the decor and the dimension, the glitter and the drama and the ambiance. I will just supply the meat and the potatoes.

First, let me present one of the all-time favorites, Helen of Troy. Imagine her being carted off by young Paris as if she is a rented television set about to be repossessed. You know how beautiful Helen is, go ahead let her be as beautiful as your envious heart can let her be. She and Paris together are so full of lust and youth and beauty and strength that even in a darkened room you would have to shield your eyes from their afterglow. And they are merely standing there, not doing a thing, just looking straight at you, holding hands just at the tips of their fingers.

When you look at the two of them this way you think that the Trojan

War may not be necessary. These two will never have the patience to make it to the gleaming ships and the wine-dark sea. They will devour each other the way the dog devours the cat in a cartoon. There will be a cloud of dust. Fur will fly. Paris will lay back and light up a Marlboro. Helen will prefigure Molly Bloom and think, "As well him as another."

Don't worry, the war will find a way to become its famous self without these lovers. But since we do have them arrested here in this pose, let's call the image of Paris and Helen the style of youth. It is marked above all by impatience, an impatience even greater than their beauty. There is also a lot of inevitability.

We are concentrating on the lovers, but I forgot to mention that all around them are the thousand ships set to go. The thousand ships all equipped with kings and crews and provisions, all just waiting for an abducted beauty to set them off. There are many bronze cups and lots of wine and barley. And in the deep background, so small and distant that you hardly see them, there are the gods. The gods are scratching one another's backs, stretching their limbs, getting ready for a little action. You look so carefully at the lovers only because of their astonishing beauty. In the story, they hardly matter.

Keep them in mind, though, if you can as I press the button for the second slide, which isn't nearly as exciting. Imagine King David, only he's not yet a king, he's actually in transit, an escapee hiding out in fear of his life. He is escaping from Saul, a mad jealous king who wants to kill him. Now this David is someone we all know. By the time we encounter him in this image (I forgot to tell you that he is hiding in a dark cave and King Saul has just entered the cave)—by this time David has, of course, lived well beyond the sweet triumph of his youth. The slaughter of Goliath was merely the beginning; in fact, that early mark of his cunning and strength has become the cause of most of David's trouble. The king wants David destroyed because he has so distinguished himself, because he is so noble, so much the people's favorite.

David has been hiding for years. He is alive largely because Saul's son, Jonathan, a true prince, has shielded David with the friendship that represents one of mankind's most splendid achievements. Thus, David at the time of our image has already killed a giant and experienced one of the most profound and disinterested friendships in history and still he is hiding in a cave as if he is a criminal. As luck or coincidence has it, his enemy, King Saul, enters that very cave in order to relieve himself.

As we all know from *Hamlet,* the time and the manner in which one kills a king is extremely important. Hamlet won't kill a king at prayer, because he fears that the king's soul would then go straight to heaven. One can hardly imagine the psychological risks that go with killing a king when he seeks privacy for a bowel movement. David, a wise man, does not risk it. David wants the crown. But in this cave that is both a toilet and a hiding place, the rules are not what they were in ancient Troy. Here, what the hero desires cannot be taken by mere strength. David has long ago experienced the victory of strength. He also has experienced being right. After all, an unjust cause would not have earned the trust and friendship of Jonathan. Thus there is no doubt that David, at the moment of this image, has justice and reason and morality on his side. He is as right to kill a king as Paris was wrong to steal a beautiful girl. In fact, in this cave King Saul is much more childlike than he is kinglike. Here, at this odd whimsical moment when the king is dethroned and the hero lurks in the shadows—here I wield the professorial dagger and label it forever, or at least for the next quarter hour—the style of middle age.

Paris, of course, would have killed Saul as surely as he ravished Helen, but still we can't jump to any easy conclusions about the differences between youth and middle age. Perhaps Paris would never have been hiding in the cave. Perhaps he would have openly claimed the throne right after he killed Goliath. Perhaps he would have been an impetuous but wise monarch who would have appointed Jonathan to administer the daily life of the kingdom while he scoured the world for demigoddesses to add dimension and joy to his seraglio.

But that would be another story, and though I am referring to imaginary slides, do not forget that all of these stationary images are always ready to burst into story at the slightest invitation. As soon as the breath of narrative touches them, these images crush the slide projector as if it were a cigarette butt and move comfortably into fiction as if they understood that the telling of stories is the central business of all our lives. This is not a profundity; it is merely a truth so obvious that everyone except the writer seems to overlook it.

There are many ways to tell our stories. Mostly we tell them as deeds—deeds, alas, so inglorious and so like the deeds of others that we all merge into the common anthill, mankind, with one big story. The subject of that single story is probably human evolution, and it is perhaps told best in what Wordsworth called "rocks and stones and trees."

Though if we could tell that story in words, if there were a poet of the DNA, the epic he could sing might make Shakespeare sound like Elvis Presley in comparison. On the other hand, such a cosmic poet might be very dull; he might be a mere reporter, a bio- and geologic Anglo-Saxon chronicler with no eye for the spiritual drama that moves through natural selection.

But telling big stories of mankind has never been any writer's subject. We writers have our hands full with a single life. Even a day, as Joyce has laboriously proved, can take five hundred pages. So we all use shortcuts. We describe the petty epiphenomena of character, things like gestures. Thus lovers "look into one another's eye"; enemies "glare"; strangers "cover their mouths and cough." And these little gestures sometimes add up to very significant events. And sometimes they happen right before our eyes. For all I know, the body language of a woman shifting in her chair at this very instant, coupled with the seductive manner in which she touches her cheek as she smothers a sneeze, may be inflaming the blood of a young man across the room. Perhaps he will go home to consult his newspaper horoscope to see if this is a good day for romance.

I will leave this promising story for others to finish. Don't forget that I abandoned David not killing the king in the cave. And I called it the style of middle age because in that image and in that story I see none of the impatience of Paris and Helen. I also notice that the gods are not surrounding the cave picking favorites and weaving destinies. By the time we see David and Saul in the cave, all of the scene-setting has already been done. Saul and David are both favorites and killing the king or not killing him are both right actions, and neither will lead to tragedy or enlightenment for David. What most impresses me about David in this instance is his patience, his tender affection, his understanding of his enemy.

In the mad uncharitable weakness of King Saul, David recognizes what he too will become, and he hesitates. It is this hesitation that I call to your attention. It is the hesitation, the uncertainty, of the style of middle age.

But even as I say this, I cannot hesitate because the nature of this topic that I have visited upon myself requires for its symmetrical conclusion one more image, an image to suggest the style of old age. This time I have selected a very snug and safe one, one that you've seen lots of times, probably in an illustrated Bible that someone gave you long ago, hoping that it would in some mysterious and wonderful way conspire with nature to make you a good person. I hope that it has worked.

The third image is the figure of Jacob wrestling with the angel. Jacob at this moment has a lot of things on his mind. He has a herd of frail cattle and sheep. He has twelve sons, two wives, and dozens of handmaidens and servants. He has just escaped after twenty years of hard labor from the house of his father-in-law, Laban, and he is about to meet his twin brother Esau for the first time since he robbed Esau of the blessing of his birthright.

We know from the story of Cain and Abel that Genesis does not paint a glowing picture of sibling rivalry. Jacob has plenty to be worried about. Esau in his youthful prime was "a wild man with his hand against every man." Who knows what he will be like after 20 years in the desert? Jacob has wisely sent ahead gifts to appease Esau: "200 she-goats and 20 he-goats, 299 ewes and 29 rams, 30 milch camels and their colts, 40 cows and 10 bulls, 20 she-asses and 10 he-asses." And even after these elaborate gifts, this peace offering, Jacob fears what Esau may do.

At precisely this moment, Jacob crosses the ford of the Jabbock River. All of his people and his possessions have crossed the stream "and Jacob was left alone; and a man wrestled with him until the breaking of the day." Symbolically and realistically, Jacob is finally alone. He has finally married his chosen wife, fathered his offspring, fulfilled his destiny. Everything he has gained in his long life is already safely across the stream. The encounter with this man will gain him neither flocks nor wives.

When at daybreak the wrestlers are still locked in indecisive combat, Jacob refuses to let the man go, even though this man has caused Jacob to limp by touching him in the hollow of his thigh. "I will not let you go," Jacob says, "unless you bless me." When he asks for a blessing, Jacob is defining the style of old age. It is a style marked not by lack of strength but by the disinterested futility of the battle. All of Jacob's worldly goods are safely across the boundary, and peace such as it can be reigns between father-in-law and son-in-law, between husband and wives, between brothers, even between men and gods. And yet for this hazy abstract non-thing, this blessing, Jacob pits himself against a divine adversary.

In this battle there literally are no stakes and yet spiritually the stakes

Max Apple

are the highest possible. Jacob wants a blessing. He who wrestles for a blessing is already beyond kingdoms and beautiful maidens. As Herman Broch suggests in his essay on old age, this is an image of art virtually dissolving into theology.

Notice that Jacob does not ask for beauty or truth or the meaning of life, notice that he asks not for wisdom or riches, he asks only for a "blessing," for a group of charged words. The understanding of those words can and does seem to be the central experience in human affairs.

For the reader it is a narrative disappointment that we do not hear the actual words of the blessing, but, in fact, all of us could provide them. We have read other blessings, we know about offspring as numerous as the sands of the earth and the stars of the heavens. These blessings Jacob already has by virtue of his fathers, by the very fact of who he is and what has already been bequeathed to him. What Jacob asks of the angel is a particular blessing appropriate to this event, to the mythic struggle of these two and only these two on this night beside the stream. What Jacob asks is the narrative distillation of this event in divine words and divine syntax and divine grammar. Jacob asks to hear the music of the spheres. And his wish is granted. He has earned it. We humble readers, we only hear the words "and there he blessed him."

Of course we desire more, but we have to be careful. Too much desire usually causes problems. Desire seems to be at the heart of the matter in all three images—desire for a woman, a kingdom, and a blessing.

This trilogy of desires reminds me of Sweeney's lines in T. S. Eliot's *Sweeney Agonistes*: "Birth and copulation and death, those are all facts when you come to brass tacks."

Eliot, I'm sure, knew better. Birth never has been a hot literary idea, though I suspect that someone, even as I write, is pecking away at the great La Maze novel.

Death is a little trickier. It seems as if death is an inevitable subject, but only if we confuse death with tragedy. They are not the same. Tragedy is the creation of death and it leaves to literature anything that literature can use—the loss, the grief, the mourning, even the renewal—but death itself does not belong to literature. It was claimed by the priests and cults thousands of years before Socrates claimed it for philosophers.

Even in the most primitive societies, "the monks in black gowns were

56

making their rounds." They took over the corpse and the rites and the mysteries, claiming for theology what no other human organization seemed any better able to claim, in ancient society or in our own time.

Yet, for all its sadness, death has always been a desirable property since it contains some of history's most valuable real estate, Heaven and Hell. Every once in a while literature makes a genuine move toward this high ground. John Milton probably made the most serious effort. But, for all Milton's genius, Billy Graham with even a modestly enthusiastic crowd probably saves more souls in a single evening than Milton has in three hundred years.

By taking tragedy but leaving death to the cults, literature was able to grow apart from theology. Yet when you glance at popular literature this may not seem so clear. Not even the Egyptian *Book of the Dead* is as gory or as pious as what lurks on the shelves of our supermarkets. There necrophiliacs display themselves right next to the weekly specials. There, dead characters speak in dead words. The masses buy these novels, I think, out of pure fear. The monstrous eyes from the cover illustrations follow us down the supermarket aisles. It's worth $2.95 to be able to shop in peace. These genre novels published under the sign of the grim reaper carve out the territory between literature and philosophy, or literature and science, or literature and theology. They specialize in the uncanny and the unknowable. They prefer black holes and the future because in those dim, cold, inhuman spaces writers can apparently get away with their dim, cold, inhuman prose.

Thus, if we leave birth to the clinicians and death to the subliterary genres, copulation is the only part of Sweeney's trilogy that is left for us. I won't quibble too much about copulation, but the word is not specific enough. We can assume that Sweeney meant by copulation the working out in time of a romance. The central question of copulation literature is when and how the lovers will couple or not couple amid many impediments and their hot desires. The literature of copulation, as many critics have pointed out, is comedy. It can, of course, turn to tragedy, as in *Romeo and Juliet,* when the complications triumph over the lovers, but much of the time, in the world and in books, couples do indeed couple. And that mingling celebrated in marriage marks the comic mode and the highlight of the style of youth.

In our slide, Paris and Helen are aglow because they are celebrating their temporary triumph. Most versions of Helen's story don't give us the details of the romance, but we can guess that it was not easy for Paris to catch Helen's eyes at a feast and speak love's words to her in the midst of many libations to the gods. It must have been enormously difficult for Paris to slip past her handmaidens and the bevy of armored heroes who seem to guard so zealously the landscape of antiquity. A modern novel would chronicle his experiences; it would, of course, be a comic novel. For even when the characters are heroes and gods, when the subject is copulation the mood tends most often to be comic.

Copulation is also one of the central motifs of the style of middle age, but in this style the question is no longer whether boy will get girl. By middle age, boy has had her and she him and both regret it. All the splendid comedy of the chase and the courtship is replaced by the gloomy sentimentality of uncoupling. For it is divorce and rebirth that occupy the high ground of the style of middle age. The style of middle age is a style of reappraisal, a style characterized by hesitation, by uncertainty, by the objects of the world rather than the passions that transport us from this world.

Yet, copulation that tyrant of youth, is still around.

Think again of David. He who hesitates to kill King Saul does not hesitate to sleep with Bath-Sheba.

Perhaps this suggests that some mythic heroes will choose to wrestle with beautiful women rather than with angels. David's middle-aged desire also suggests what we knew even in youth, that the biologic necessity driving us to couple does not with the same violent grace thrust us toward serenity and wisdom.

When one hesitates, when one examines, he usually finds things a little unsatisfactory, even himself. When Socrates said that the unexamined life was not worth living, he was writing the motto of the style of middle age. Youth does not examine itself. We know this from our own lives as well as from history and literature.

Consider, again, Paris chasing Helen in Menelaus' city. Imagine Paris in the midst of his overwhelming passion stopping to think about Helen's shady ancestry. Imagine the two of them planning to grow old together. Had they looked up even for a moment they could have seen the ships, the kings, the armies, the big tragedy waiting to overtake them.

Had Helen stopped to say good-bye to her handmaidens, to look ruefully over her possessions, to cast sad glances at the stony land-scape of her marriage, we would be in the territory of the style of middle age, a style characterized much more by sentimentality than by the de-sire of the moment.

But, if we think of the style of middle age as exclusively a chronologi-cal and biological function, we are missing its subtlety. It can happen at any time but is located somewhere in the range between stealing the beautiful girl and risking everything for an abstract blessing. The Bil-dungsroman, the story of growing up, after awhile ceases to be enough. As Dr. Johnson reminds us, "The old man does not want the young man's whore." Our hormones, halfway between Romeo and Juliet and Rabbi Ben Ezra, look up figuratively from their dingy abode in the grinding business of making life; they give the brain a pause to consider the busi-ness of observing life. The reflective gaze, beginning at the genitals, moves from the genitals constantly away from the body, away even from ambition and greed. In the example I have been using, we might say that the reflective range of style moves from the face of Helen, where it sets the world aflame, to the groin of Jacob, where it is merely a minor wound. But for a while the gaze stays fixed in this world, somewhere slightly above the genitals but nowhere near the angels. The gaze looks past the human form, over the shoulder perhaps. It stays fixed long enough for the style to take in the fullness of social life as it has in *Middlemarch* or in *One Hundred Years of Solitude,* where the key organism becomes a town or a family line and the characters, for all their individual interests, become submerged into something much larger. In a way this style of middle age is a movement toward what Marxists call the "typical" without any of the Marxist baggage. When copulation loses her rough hold, when we have come near to the end of our reproductive lives, we hesi-tate. When we look past the body, we don't know what we'll find. Similarly, we can almost watch the careers of our novelists as they move often from the comic encounter of youth to the sentimentalities of middle age and only rarely to the sublime abstract.

If the style of youth is much concerned with the possession of the loved one, the style of middle age is much concerned with things, with objects. It tends to be a very fat style. Henry James, who is one of the modern monarchs of this style once wrote a novel about furniture, *The Spoils of Poynton.* I hate to lump Henry James with all those contemporary novels about hotels and airports and millionaires and models, but the style of middle age encompasses all those lengthy prose descriptions of things and people.

It does so under the heading of "realism," which is the password of the style of middle age. Realism gives us the masonry of everyone's daily life. I confess that I don't like it. It is one of the big drawbacks of the style of middle age. When I encounter too much of it, I rarely have a nice day. The style of youth, for all its narrowness, is often pithy and direct. Nathaniel West is the American writer whom I most admire in this style. His subject is always disillusion; the dreams of art, love, religion and beauty all go "pop" in his sentences. He writes grenades going off disguised as champagne bubbles, but in his clear, thin, lucid style he never lets the reader get sentimental about the bubbles.

In our image of the youthful style, Paris is the man of action. His art— his whole art—is action, pure and immediate, animal-like, leaving the consequences for others. It is not a style that is endearing, and the mess it leaves is usually where the style of middle age begins. That is, the best story of the Trojan War, and indirectly of Helen and Paris, is not about the war or these lovers but about Odysseus and the way that he goes about reclaiming his life from the mess that others have brought upon him.

So, just as the style of youth makes the mess in its quick and energetic way, the style of middle age is left to catalog the mess and wallow in the problem youth has created. And this is where most of our so-called mature work lies. This stuck-in-the-mud sentimentality is the most profound flaw of the style of middle age. Old age knows that there is only a blessing, perhaps, and youth, as Walt Whitman says, understands that there is only "a suck and a sell," a beauty to be conquered. The style of middle age encompasses the whole solemn, silly, hopeless, necessary business of trying to make some sense out of the world.

The style of middle age, the attempt to make sense of the mess, has moved in the past two hundred years from double combat to single.

The easiest way to clear things up used to be the duel. From Homer right through Pushkin, dueling is a clean and handy device. But in our century we have begun to experience satisfaction by understanding rather than by dueling. The field of battle has moved inside the self. The simple old-fashioned duel has been replaced by psychoanalysis, so that we can now win or lose and then worry about it forever after.

I could go on making all kinds of generalizations, but allow me instead to illustrate from my own brief glide through the style of youth. As you can see, I have turned the corner of middle age. In most kinds of work a 41-year-old lazy male with bad eyesight would hardly qualify as young and promising. Yet the odd and bumpy apprenticeship of literature often consumes so much time and energy that by the time we reach the style of youth our own youth is long gone. I hope you see that by the style of youth I do not mean juvenilia. What I here call the style of youth is certainly not artless, and it includes not only Hemingway and Nathaniel West but Isaac Babel and Jonathan Swift and Henry Fielding and almost all the satirists you can think of. So to come to the style of youth at any age is a very significant achievement.

I took the long way to style: I didn't take the advice of the muse to look in my heart and write: I went to school. There I learned that the novel was dead. I learned that it had been a loose baggy monster and that someone had finally shot it up. I guess it was a whole group of hunters, the new critics. They sniffed it out and gunned it down. They really had no choice, you see, because early in the century Henry James had labeled it and James Joyce had undressed it and D. H. Lawrence had sodomized it. So the new critics had to take it out of its misery.

The novel has been dying a long graceless death and some of us have been called maggots feeding on the dying carcass. I'm not so sure about any of this. Perhaps I live so close that I don't notice the stench. I can only tell you that when I finally got to it, the rotting hulk of fiction seemed very lively to me. I was happy to have at it.

I came to it carrying my lunch and a letter of introduction from my grandmother and about two dozen stories that I had carefully dipped in everyday language until they shined without waxing or buffing. I was looking for a good spot in the house of fiction, just a little place where I could make myself comfortable and get cozy, you know, the way pushcart entrepreneurs looked for a place on busy streets early in this century.

Though it might have been long dead when I got to it, the corpus of fiction was still a crowded and active place. There was plenty going on. I headed for some of the major neighborhoods, the places I had read about. First I went toward the milk of human kindness, but Donald Barthelme was already spaciously camped out there, drinking it up and spitting it away. Just to his left I saw William Gass feeding on the holiness of the heart's affection, and then I began to realize that I might have some difficulty finding my place. I went to John Barth, who at that time was the neighborhood leasing agent, but he could only take applications for nine hundred square pages and over. He was exceptionally polite but left me to my own devices to find a place.

Everywhere I looked there was astonishing activity. A little extra confusion at that time was caused by a group of French anthropologists who were doing a topographic map of the life of the mind, but apart from their loud and incessant questions in ungrammatical English, there was a lot of internal strife among the residents. All of the writers were fighting over the anus, Nabakov had completed staking out the tongue, and Philip Roth had the penis. Everyone jealously guarded his territory. I looked for the female parts but there were none. The photographers, I learned, had turned them all into flowers. A band of female writers was busy resurrecting genitalia out of memory and resentment and bitterness but Leslie Fiedler stood beside them, telling them that they had no place on this body. He was trying to sell them tickets to France, but the females, having looked at the French anthropologists, had decided to make their stand over here.

I lost all track of time so I can't tell you how long I roamed along this lively dead novel, but I felt as if I had taken the grand tour of Europe in the sidecar of a motorcycle. It was so bumpy and uncertain for me that I couldn't appreciate all I was seeing. Finally I found a place. It was under the left middle fingernail, an aging subdivision called "Jewish, Jewish-American, not so Jewish and not so American either."

It was one of the nosiest sectors on the body, but I slipped in and found a place that had been vacated when the inhabitant moved to Hollywood. As crowded and argumentative as the subdivision was, I was relieved to have finally found my own place, but it was very hard to sleep.

At night, the men who held down some of the major neighborhoods came to our section to kibbitz and argue. Mailer, Bellow, Singer, Malamud, Roth—they all liked to spend their evenings in the old neighborhood, but they didn't leave their territories unguarded. When they came to us they each appointed a gentile watchman from the *New York Review of Books* to make sure nobody bothered their settlements.

There was so much squabbling in our little neighborhood that we finally had to organize and respect seniority and authority. We agreed on seniority but we gave authority only to the dead. So, by popular vote, we elected Martin Buber and Sholem Alecheim to be our representatives to the body politic and to give us each our assignments.

Since I had so little seniority, they assigned me teeth and foreskins. I could have left, could have just quit right after that miserable assignment and gone to Hollywood or academic life or the law, but I had already put in such a long apprenticeship that I decided to stick it out.

And that, of course, is what I've been doing for almost a decade, making what I can out of teeth and foreskins. This assignment has kept me in the periphery of the big house, but whenever I approach any of the major places, those watchmen are there telling me to go back to my zany and clever assignments.

But I'm here to confess that I have fooled them. I learned that teeth and foreskins are very significant. It's all a matter of perspective.

In the style of youth, all you can do is joke about an assignment like mine, and most of the jokes are very stale, except once in a while you get a masterpiece out of such humble territory—look at what Gogol did with a nose or Victor Hugo with a hunchback, or Hawthorne with a birthmark. In the style of middle age you begin to learn that the old timers, even Homer and King David, dabbled in your neighborhood.

Homer, as is fitting for a military writer, thought of teeth as an ultimate defense, the last line of defense against the most crucial mistakes, mistakes of language. Once a phrase has crossed what Homer calls "the teeth's barrier," there is no recalling it. Achilles says that he won't rejoin the battle and there you have the tragedy. If only his teeth had clamped down on the fateful words as emphatically as the goddess grabbed his arm when he was reaching for his sword to slay Agamemnon. But the goddess paid no attention to words, to the teeth's barrier. It must be from the gods that we learn that "actions speak louder than words," although this is not always so.

The capture of foreskins, like the capture of weapons or scalps or any other booty, suggests the power of the conqueror. But for David the power of the conqueror sits ironically upon him. He saw the follies of Saul; he knew that the state he desired was peace, but peace eluded him. He moved to the style of middle age very rapidly after his conquest of Goliath and yet David continued to act out his necessary role as the warrior king, a role that culminated in his adultery with Bath-Sheba.

Just as Paris and Helen are the clear emblems of the style of youth, so

David and Bath-Sheba are the hazy emblems of the style of middle age. No dramatic thunderclaps follow their adultery and nothing like the Trojan War ensues. Bath-Sheba's husband, Uriah the Hittite, a decent man, dies in battle. The first child of David and Bath-Sheba dies seven days after his birth. This infant's death is a domestic event, a sad private event in the almost wholly public life of the king and psalmist. The shepherd boy who begins the style of his middle age by not killing Saul defiles the reflective style by his lust for Bath-Sheba. Because David never wholly lives in the hesitant, safe, accumulating style of middle age, he has no chance to approach the subtlety and sublimity of the style of old age, the style of an Odysseus who knows what it means to return from battle. Thus it is that the fruition of David's style of middle age happens not in his lifetime but in the long, peaceful, and wise rule of his son Solomon—Solomon, who is, ironically, the son of Bath-Sheba.

You have probably noticed that I am choosing to speak mostly about those works that we call "ageless" or "timeless." No doubt these phrases are meant to suggest that the stories I am referring to are continually "fresh," as fresh as the vegetables in your grocer's freezer, or as "absorbing" as his cellulose sponges. In fact, the strength of the stories comes from their staleness and their antiquity. For fresh and absorbing tales you will have to go elsewhere. The essence of the style of middle age is what King Solomon engraved on his ring: "This too shall pass." You know that you are in the midst of something that will leave, something that is neither fresh nor absorbing, but something persistent.

To chronicle that persistence, mankind for centuries has turned to a kind of legal language or prose. If in fact Socrates is right and philosophy *is* the study of death, then literature is surely a long course in learning how to write one's will.

Let me then end this examination of style with a modest appendage, my first literary will and testament:

I affirm that I believe myself to be of sound mind and hope that after reading this you will agree and bear witness.

Whatever objects I have acquired are of only temporary interest and I bequeath these, of course, to my heirs.

But the writer's true wealth cannot be measured in objects. What wealth I have is measured in the tin scale of irony.

Therefore, I bequeath to all the apprentices who are striving now after the hot muse of youth, photography. And if this new art is not enough for their ambitions, I'll gladly throw in psychology too—dreams, nightmares, the steamy groves of the unconscious and whatever is left of the model of sweet reason.

To the scientists I bequeath the engineers; may they rule over them with a mighty hand, though I doubt it.

To the philosophers I bequeath the French anthropologists, the constructors and the deconstructors, the old new critics and the new new critics.

But to you, gentle readers, unsystematic gropers, and patient watchers of the world, to you I bequeath the confusion of the crowded comic strip and, above all, the clear black line that separates one image from another. To you I leave the three images I have described and whatever you can make of them. To you I leave a passionate interest in the trivia of your own lives and times, a deep satisfaction in all the insignificant glances you will collect, all the uncataloged gestures and feelings that will come your way. I leave to you an appreciation of all your lively clichés and those of your politicians and sportscasters and lovers. I ask only on behalf of myself and my humble colleagues of the future that when you are through with your trivial deeds and words, you will be so kind as to put them outside as neatly bagged as your trash. For we writers are constantly making our rounds. As invisibly as microwaves, we go from house to house, often while you sleep, collecting all the observations you don't need. We take all of this stuff home. We mix two parts narcissism to one part melancholy, add a little dash of imagination and let it bake for half a lifetime. When the product emerges, you often don't recognize it, though sometimes you buy it because it looks familiar.

Yes, we're out there, always recycling the stuff you don't need, sifting it through our own yeasty experiences, transforming it always, selling it sometimes.

I bequeath it to you with all my good wishes and with the full understanding that you might reduce it to a message and beat it into a cliché, and then give it back. When you do give it back, it goes straight to the junk pile, the very one in which I found Helen of Troy, King David and Jacob. At any age, in any style, that's the best place to look.

George Garrett

How to Do the Literary

Speaking of Minor Revelations
(David and Goliath)

What could be virtue in a giant
is rashness in small boys. The point
beyond which childhood is
calamity is clearly marked.

The giant, standing like a bear,
must be astounded, raise a roar
of natural indignation or
tilt to laugh at the improbable.

So they must always meet that way,
be disciplined and neat as puppets.
So I must always praise,
with brutal innocence, the accidental.

He's lucky who dies laughing
in the light of it, who leaves
the deft philosophers to argue
that excess is illumination.

Some verses from the middle 1940s, probably 1946, with me, or anyway the stranger to me now who bore my name then, being either 16 or 17 years old. Someone with my name then, not looking much like me now, and in many ways a complete stranger, save that now, having lived long-er than he dared to imagine possible, or could if he had cared to, having changed more, inwardly and outwardly, than his imagination or brief bright flashes of prescience would (fortunately) allow him to endure in advance—now I can understand not himself but at least some of the reasons why the story of David and Goliath was an appealing and enig-matic figure for a number of things in and about life and art, not all of them ineffable. It was (now that I think of it) always about style. Among other things, David's remarkable disposal of Goliath with his sling and found stones has always seemed to me an action that was at once su-premely stylish and superbly inappropriate. As for Real Life . . . consider that I had (though I had no way of knowing this for certain) just con-cluded a brief and utterly foolish and absolutely hopeless, not com-pletely unsuccessful career—I only lost one fight, the last one, after all—as a middleweight fighter, never a contender, and was about to go off to college where my next best main aim and goal was to be a football player. I emerged from the experience of fighting my betters, all of them significantly taller than I, not wiser or much more skilled at it than I had begun, but with a nose that had been broken many times and with teeth that had been shattered one and all to the roots, (and here I am smiling with them, most of them, still) and I could go away at any time without a mark or scar on my face to show for it. Without applying the lesson spe-cifically to myself, I had learned to be wary of people with unmarked, unscarred faces. I had moved on to play briefly at being a genuine David upon a field full of Goliaths, ruining both knees, breaking both feet, cov-ering my body with cloudy bruises, but more or less holding my own until the arrival of the face mask as a part of the conventional required equip-ment ruined the one great equalizer that a short squat pulling guard and middle linebacker could depend on, namely the fact that nobody, be he ever so big, enormous, gigantic, and huge, likes to get his nose broken and his teeth knocked out. Flying elbows worked no wonders against a face mask. After that, I recollect only long afternoon hours in the steam and stink of a training room and myself hobbling back to the dormitory as swaddled in tape, head to toe, as any decently dressed mummy, reeking of a medley of salves and linaments, groaning (quietly, quietly, smile fixed on face lest anyone suspect my pain) as I passed the tennis courts where crowds of young men all in white and all of them trim and handsome and graceful, not Goliaths, nary a one, but every one an F. Scott Fitzgerald (this was, after all, Princeton); they flaunted what I had to admit was style. I can still hear, at grim will, the keen, crisp sound of tennis balls and rackets meeting each other in the autumnal air, can still summon up the slow-fading afternoon light, the scent of woodsmoke from somewhere, likewise leafsmoke—for they still burned their leaf piles in those days. And in the midst of it all, a boy mummy who would cheerfully have leapt into a burning leaf pile if he could have vanished with the thick, pale gray smoke of it . . . but didn't. Vanished instead, eventually, into the U.S. Army, as a perennial enlisted man, where he learned well how an outward and visible obedient humility can aptly disguise an inward and spiritual exile and cunning. Where he lost the brutal innocence of the aforesaid poem.

As for the poem's style: I can't imagine where it came from, though it certainly seems to suit the fellow who wrote it and who, in his arrogant innocence, would never have imagined himself here and now in such excellent and reputable company, but who also, I must admit in all wistful fairness, wouldn't have cared a whit, one way or the other, if he had been told to expect it. For this to matter at all (and it does matter & I'm grateful to be included here, after all) it was necessary that the arrogant and ignorant innocence be lost, as it was bound to be, and that years of enforced outward and visible humility should slowly teach him a little more cunning, enough to save his skin if not his soul.

A little later "Speaking of Minor Revelations" was in a book with a company of cousin poems, a book that nobody much liked but Miss Marianne Moore. But that was enough, and she was more than enough for someone who had not (yet), by dint of worldly instruction in humility, joined the man in the ditch waiting for a charitable Samaritan to pass by. The style changed, and yet the next decade, the 1950s, found me— found *him,* I mean—still thinking about David and Goliath, still trying, then, to come to terms with disproportion, still seeking a language and a voice that together could contain both the young shepherd and the giant, the outward and the inward. . . .

> *Giant Killer*
>
> I've heard the case for clarity. I know
> much can be said for fountains and for certain bells

that seem to wring the richness from the day
like juice of sweetest fruits, say, plums and tangerines,
grapes and pineapples and peaches. There are so many
ripe things, crushed, will sing on the thrilled tongue.

I know the architecture of the snow's composed
of multitudes of mirrors whose strict forms
prove nothing if they do not teach that God loves all
things classic, balanced and austere in grace
as, say, Tallchief in *Swan Lake,* a white thing floating
like the feather of a careless angel, dropped.

But there are certain of God's homely creatures that
I can love no less—the shiny toad, a fine hog fat in the mud,
sporting like Romans at the baths, a mockingbird
whose true song is like oboes out of tune, a crow
who, cawing above a frozen winter field,
has just the note of satire and contempt.

I will agree that purity's a vital matter,
fit for philosophers and poets to doze upon. I'll agree
the blade is nobler than a rock. But then I think
of David and Goliath, how he knelt
and in a cloudy brook he felt for stones.
I like that disproportion. They were well thrown.

David (from Abraham's Knife)

I think Caravaggio has seen it right,
shown, anyway, with the boy and the head
(Is it really his own face, the giant's
slack-jawed, tormented? Another story . . .)
the look of the lean boy, the lips
pursed to spit or kiss, the head held high
at arm's length from him by the hair,
the eyes, if they show anything, revealing
pity and contempt, hatred and love,
the look we keep for those we kill.
He will be king. Those fingers twined
in dark will pluck the hair of harps,

golden to make the music of our joy
and anguish. By hair will Absalom
dangled from a limb, his tongue a thoroughfare
for flies, and this man grown old and soft
will tear his from the roots to make lament.
The look you give Goliath on that day
will flicker in your filmy eyes again
when you spy bare Bathsheba on the roof
(O dark honey, liquor of strange flesh,
to turn a head to birds, a heart to stone!)
and you will live to learn by heart
the lines upon this alien face.
So I am saying Caravaggio
saw it right, that at the moment when
the boy has killed the man and lifts the head
to look at it is the beginning and the end.
I, who have pictured this often and always
stopped short of ending, seen David stoop
and feel for smooth stones in the cloudy brook,
the instant when his palm and fist
close like a beggar's on a cold coin,
know now I stopped too soon.
Bathed in light, this boy is bound
to be a king. But the sword . . .
I had forgotten that. A slant
of brightness, its fine edge rests
across his thigh. Never gain a rock will do.
It fits his hand like a glove.

In the 1960s, the boy and I fell among thieves and committed more prose than anything else. I had begun to publish stories and a couple of novels in the 1950s, prose works that, in the southern tradition, celebrated the vernacular even as they sought to explore it. The epigraph for my first book of stories, taken from the *Octavian* of Minucius Felx, says it all: *Non loquimur magna sed vivimus.* We do not speak greatly, but we live. That was my hope even as it was an assertion. But in the 1960s, I begin to give way to groaning, though I could grit my teeth in the semblance of a proper grin. I gave way to the vernacular, leaped upon the smoldering leaf pile and produced a number of things, including this next little piece on style that comes to us from and through an odd character named John Towne, about whom a word or two may be helpful if not really necessary. . . . If the serpent bites before it is charmed, there is no advantage in a charmer (Ecclesiastes 10:11).

John Towne is essentially a wicked man, as worthless as Confederate money, as useless and outdated as a celluloid collar. Unfortunately, he is also the protagonist of a novel I have been working on (against my better judgment and the judgment of my betters) for a very long time. No matter what I try to do, no matter how insulting I am, he will not get lost. However, it appears that I'll have the last laugh on him because (a) it seems highly unlikely that the novel will ever be finished; (b) even if I do accidentally finish it, I am confident that no self-respecting American publisher would ever publish it. Let's hope not. Towne has no redeeming social interest. He couldn't care less. And what makes it really bad is that he is a would-be writer. He is always *expressing* himself. If you'll pardon the expression. . . .

Anyway, here is an example of Towne in action with his battered Olivetti and his dreams of glory. It's a mere fragment, of course. That's Towne's *genre*—the fragment. Fortunately for the health of American letters, he has never been able to finish anything. This subversive lecture was apparently prepared by Towne to deliver to his innocent students at a college where, briefly and under false credentials, he held a teaching job. It is uncertain precisely what college that may have been. (Towne refers to it as Nameless College, VA, in the hope that he will never get around to delivering the lecture there or anywhere else.)

Draft for a Lecture on How to Achieve and
Maintain a Modern Prestigious Literary Style

Now if you want to sound poetic and literary and all at the same time, always remember to get the show on the road with a big, fat, easygoing dependent clause, holding off the subject for a good while and letting your participles and your adjectives do the heavy work for you. Hold back on the verb for as long as you possibly can. Otherwise it can end up being as embarrassing and rhetorically as disappointing as premature ejaculation. Moreover, this particular method serves to generate a certain suspense. Which can be a great help. Particularly if your story doesn't really have any in the first place. Also it sounds like you have read a trunk load of foreign books in their original languages.

Here I have put together a very stylish sentence as an example. Of course, it suffers from being no more (and no less) than a hastily constructed *pastiche*. But, nevertheless, I reckon it will have to do.

Here's how it goes:

"Bemused and even perhaps vaguely mysterious behind the smooth *café au lait* of an unseasonal suntan, the colonel, clutching his invisible but nonetheless palpable enigma gracefully about him like a marshal's splendid cape. . . ."

And next, right here, is where the verb should come along.

Let's take a look at it. Point of view. We are observing the colonel from the outside, from a sort of camera angle. That's good. And there is an ambiguity about this civilized lens. Which is also good, in fact very good. Ambiguity is almost always a good thing in our line of work. In fact, the narrator-observer merely tosses these perceptions gracefully aside. He's got a million of 'em. Or so it seems.

Notice the use of *café au lait*. Words in italics that, upon closer inspection, turn out to be words or phrases in some foreign language that the average lazybones may fairly be expected to know (or anyway recognize) at sight tend to look good on the page and add some status appeal. They serve to join the reader and the observer-narrator in a spontaneous, yet exclusive club for slightly world-weary travellers.

Unseasonal suntan is a stroke of genius, if I do say so myself. There it is, just lying there in the big middle of the sentence like a candy wrapper or a crumpled kleenex by the roadside. Yet it contrives to tell us a whole lot about the colonel. To begin with, consider this: *he has got a tan at the wrong time of the year.* He probably uses a sunlamp and probably looks in the mirror a lot. Or maybe he is always sneaking off to Florida or the Virgin Islands or Barbados or somewhere else like that when he ought to be home and working for a living like everybody else. In any case, he is either a victim of his own stupid arrogance or bad taste or both. Metaphorically, which is on the all-important second level, this teeny little clue lets us know that he may very well be a bad guy. I mean, he is not natural. He is a phony. Sun is good and good for you. Everybody knows that. People who love the sun and get good natural suntans—excluding, of course, all those people and races of mankind who seem to be stuck with permanent suntans of one shade and the other and who, in most modern and contemporary fiction, are definitely presumed to be good until it is irrefutably proved otherwise—people who don't blister or peel or ever have to rub themselves with Noxema, sun people are good people. We all know that. It is an article of faith.

But mark this well, readers. This cat, this dude, this jive turkey colonel with his suntan, he is coming on like he is one of the good people. Like real, honest-to-God, fun-loving, mankind-and-nature-loving, right-thinking, liberal, sun-loving people. And chances are we might not be able to distinguish him from the real distinguished thing. Except, dear hearts, for that jewel of an adjective—*unseasonal*. Which our otherwise more or less neutral and objective observer-narrator has tossed like a gold coin or a piece of cake into the unruly mob of words. And by that adjective alone we who know our modern lit. from peanut butter are at least entitled to suspect that he may be a bad guy who has swiped somebody else's white hat. Oh, he will probably fool some of the characters in this story, especially the slow-witted ones; but we, as ever alert and suspicious readers, shall remain faithfully on our guard.

Now notice some of the other key words—*bemused, mysterious, enigma,* etc. While receiving the observer-narrator's basic signal— "Beats me what's bugging the Bird Colonel"—we are also getting a side dish of literary class. And we can relax and be safely assured that our observer-narrator has at least carefully gone through *Thirty Days To A More Powerful Vocabulary.* He is definitely a literary type; for (ask anyone) *bemused* is one of your gold-plated, definitely okay New Yorker–type literary words.

Note the adverbs. Which are sparingly and judiciously used. Frequent use of adverbs implies a very high degree of intelligence and sophistication. For example, in fiction your average upper-class British character may be expected to throw his adverbs around like they are fixing to go out of style the day after tomorrow. This is also true of those Americans who have been to school at Oxford or Cambridge or would like to sound like they might have. As a practical exercise you should count the number of adverbs found in any *New Yorker* story or article, picked at random. You'll see. Chances are you'll find a swarm of adverbs anywhere you look.

But let us not sit here smugly and rest content with easy observation. After all, no matter how stylish and decorative it may be, an adverb is still a functional part of speech. Among a number of other things, an adverb usually qualifies the action of a verb. To qualify something is to divert attention away from the thing in and of itself; that is, away from the action. An abundance of adverbs can bring all the action to a screeching, shuddering halt. Please remember that all action is, *per se*, vulgar and commonplace. Or put it another way. You may pick your nose in public if you must. But always try to do it with style. Do it with an adverb.

Moreover, since adverbs are, in a sense, the traveling salesmen of style, they tend always to make a persuasive case for style even without seeming to be hustling. Let us suppose, just for the sake of example, that you were a writer with absolutely nothing to say—John Updike, for example. Would you confess to your problem and quit writing? Hell no, you wouldn't. By the shrewd and judicious use of all the shell-game devices of style, you could give content and substance the middle finger and just keep on writing the same old crap forever and ever.

Be that as it may, please permit me to call your attention to another artistic touch, almost the equal of the brilliant use of *unseasonal*. I am referring to the clause that reads "clutching an invisible but nonetheless palpable enigma gracefully about him like a marshal's splendid cape. . . ." Now that one is a honey, a real humdinger. That one little word, *clutching*, speaks volumes. Let's be honest with ourselves. Let's face it. To clutch anything is to be very crude. Clutching, like a number of other forms of grasping, is associated with greed. Also with all kinds of unseemly urgency and boring desperation. It conjures up a sordid world of ridiculous social climbers who are not to the manner born. If you get my meaning. Don't be fooled for even a minute by all that "invisible" but nonetheless palpable "enigma" stuff. This colonel is not only most likely some kind of a phony, he is also running scared. He is obviously terrified of something. On the other hand, please do not feel that the other characters in the situation are necessarily low-grade morons or retards just because they can't see through the colonel. You shouldn't expect them to be as smart and as sensitive as our narrator-observer, who appears to be willing to share some of his *apercus* with us. Art isn't all that simple. Many times Art will fake you right out of your shoes. Art will leave you standing there, sucking wind and wondering how you ever got into this mess.

Sure he is *clutching* his *enigma*. Why not? Wouldn't you be if you had one? But never mind. The really important thing is, of course, how he is clutching it. Like a lady with a towel when the friendly plumber barges into the bathroom without knocking? Like an old man with a shawl when he feels a chilly draft? Like a miser with a dollar bill? Like a jack pine high up near timberline on the sheer edge of a cliff? Like Harold Lloyd on a window ledge? Like King Kong holding Fay Wray? No, no, a thousand times no! I mean the man tells us how—"like a marshal's splendid cape." Not Herbert Marshall or E. G. Marshall or R. G. Marshall or General Marshall. Just a marshal, any old marshal. *Gracefully,* too. Graceful is good. Clumsy and awkward are bad. Graceful is what your basic good, natural, liberal, suntanned people usually turn out to be.

Now, then, the cape.

Ask yourself—and I mean this seriously—when is the last time, outside of some old movies, you have actually seen a marshal's cape. For that matter, when is the last time you have actually encountered a marshal. (I here exclude federal marshals.) There are marshals and marshals. Know what I mean? There is old Marshal Tito, for example, an ambivalent character. There are Hitler's marshals. They were very bad. Except some people like Marshal Rommel, the Desert Fox. Napoleon had marshals, too. Who cares if they were bad or good? Nobody really knows or can remember. Nevertheless, they were French. And they are now long since dead and gone to dust or glory. So, as dead Frenchmen, they can now be glorious, romantic, dashing, brave, doomed, impeccable, splendid, etc.

And thus we are getting the old double whammy. Maybe this colonel is the Hitler type. Or maybe he is Napoleonic. Frankly, I incline toward the former view on the strength of that unseasonal suntan and the clutching going on. But only time and a couple of hundred pages will tell for sure. And during that time and those pages we must always allow for the possibility that the aforesaid colonel may change for the better or the worse; or stay pretty much the same; or get dropped out of the story and forgotten about. Anything (or nothing) can happen.

I shall not trouble you by calling attention to such minor and felicitous technicalities as rhythm, assonance and dissonance, alliteration, symmetrical balance, parallelism, and so on, except to point out that they are all in there, and plenty of them too. Notice that you are approximately halfway through the sentence (go right ahead and count if you want to), all the way up to that word *suntan,* before you even have a clue what the subject of the sentence is.

Is it a bird?

Is it a plane?

Is it Vanessa Redgrave?

Suspense mounts steadily to reach a peak at *suntan.*

"Ah! It's the colonel," we say. "I wonder what the old fart is up to."

Then you have to wait all the way through the second half of the sentence to find out.

Don't hold your breath.

Sooner or later a verb will come winging on in and land safely. Just like in German or Latin. Do you remember those good old high school Latin exercises? "Then having saluted and having bade farewell to the centurion, from the north gate riding forth, the south gate being sorely beset by the barbarians, the messenger the letter from the commander's hand to the Emperor bravely sought to carry."

Or let's try one in Kraut: "Hans Schmerz in the Black Forest during April near the charming village of Horsford was born."

Point is, see, if you can screw up an English sentence sufficiently, you can pass for a college graduate.

Although it is absent from my own sentence, the verb nevertheless important and relevant will prove to be. Now then, your average writer, who might be called a run-of-the-mill, blue-collar stylist, could probably get that far, huffing and puffing. And then he would probably blow the whole thing sky-high by introducing an inappropriate verb. Consider what things the colonel may possibly do and still not violate the context, decorum, dramatical architecture and syntactical construction.

What if he:

(a) took off like a big-ass bird?

(b) burped, belched, barfed, and blew lunch?

(c) whistled "Pop Goes the Weasel"?

(d) farted as loud as a slide trombone?

(e) made himself a peanut butter and jelly sandwich?

(f) grinned and whinnied like a jackass chewing briars?

(g) crossed his eyes and fluttered his tongue in a loud Bronx cheer?

(h) lit up an exploding cigar?

(i) picked his teeth with a rusty nail?

(j) dropped his trousers and threw a bald moon at everyone standing behind him?

I shall spare you by ending this list that is already threatening to grow to epic proportions. From here on, you will just have to take my word for it. In point of fact, there are only two things in the whole world that the colonel can actually do.

He can cough discreetly.

Or he can smile.

I like to think that under the circumstances he may have smiled. Because smiles are more ambiguous than coughs.

The point is that real style is very hard to do. And it gets harder and harder all the time. Everybody keeps jumping in and trying to get into the act. For instance, all the good shiny prestige words keep getting snatched up by politicians and newspaper writers and cheap and grubby advertising types. Why, those people can take anything, even a nice, clean, crisp. ordinary word, one that we all know and love and use all the time, and in no time at all it will be filthy and soiled beyond any saving.

Faced with the pitiful and constant corruption and debasement of his native tongue, the average American writer can only do what he has always done before and emphatically return to the strength and energy, the indecorous and often unbalanced vitality of the living and breathing and spoken vernacular. And just hope for the best. . . .

(From here on just keep winging until the bell rings.)

    J.T.

Came then the 1970s and I, George Garrett, moved on to different places, to new pastures. And I rid myself of Towne by sending him off to Africa disguised as an Episcopalian clergyman—the Reverend R. P. King, his first initial discretely disguising a first name taken out of the southern vernacular tradition—Radio. He's a twin, Towne is, and his daddy named his brother Philco in honor of that wonderful, glowing cathedral shape around which the whole family so often huddled in the evening, listening to distant worlds.

Anyway, he was gone and I said (and still say) good riddance, except that n'er-do-well and inwardly shriveled individual did in truth teach me something about how a character, real or imaginary, can create a style. And next came forth another kind of character, someone I had been wrestling with, as Jacob wrestled his angel to earn a scar and learn his name, ever since the early 1950s—Sir Walter Raleigh, a giant inwardly and outwardly (he was six and a half feet tall, which may not be nearly so rare now as then, but remains noteworthy). When he decides to speak of style, in *Death of the Fox,* it is in the form of an imaginary letter to his real son and heir, Carew, and this letter (later to be burned for the sake of verisimilitude) begins with the abandonment of one kind of style for another.

My son, it is the prerogative of the old to inflict upon the young and tedious celebration of the past, spent seasons, festivals, and holidays of lost time. And as the world goes, it falls the duty of the young to hear them out or to seem to; and remains the privilege of the old to practice that prerogative, though the exercise serve only to prove the folly thereof. For the old hold no patent, license, or monopoly on wisdom, which, being mysterious and, all reasonable men agree, invaluable, is beyond the possession of one man or another, one station or one age. For youth, though bound to ignorance out of inexperience, is not likewise condemned to be foolish. For if the purpose of the old be to transmit such wisdom as they deem they have come into, together with a history of themselves and their experience, judiciously framed and arranged in quiet afterthought, and thereby to preserve for the young the best of what has been, and so to defend them from the repetition of many errors and follies of the past, then their intent is surely foolish. It is doomed and fated to fail. The young will either listen, nodding assent and masking an honest indifference, thus learning chiefly the fine art of duplicity at a tender age, or they will listen truly, but without full understanding; as newly arrived in a foreign country, one listens out of courtesy, and with much frowning concentration, to a strange tongue, the grammar of which is less than half mastered. Or, should a young man be fortunate enough to be free from need to listen to elders or heed the clucking of old ganders, whose chief claim to excellence is to have lived long enough to be unfit for anything except a stewing pot, he will stop his ears or walk away in insolence, leaving an old man to mutter at his own shadow by the fire.

Nonetheless, with knowledge of the vanity of my purpose and some foreknowledge of its likely failure, I would seek. . . .

I would seek . . . what?

A clumsy exercise in antiquated style, lacking the time for revision and polish; so that even if I were not to be credited for any substance whatsoever, I might win grudging approval for virtuosity.

Time will bleed away, an inward wound, until I truly bleed.

If time were blood and an executioner struck off my head now, there would be nothing left in me for a crowd to see. A drained and cured carcass only. For I have been gutted and cleaned and hung up by time like a pig in the cellar. They say— do they not?—that I have the pig's eye. Just so. . . . I can find no fault now with that. What is gossip may sometimes be poetry.

"Old men are twice children," the proverb says. Perhaps my son will bear with me for the sake of my second childhood.

You will have noticed that, even as I was bending over my desk writing that down, I was growing as old as Sir Walter Raleigh. Even as I have grown old together with my black and tan hound dog, James, named for the last King of the Scots alone. And now this second time I have just looked up from my desk and the task at hand to find myself and the whole world ten years older and shabbier and worse for wear, my old dog full of yawns and sleep, my children grown up and myself (except for this present shining moment here and now, where I confess that my colleagues, male and female, seem to me as bright and cheerfully glamorous as any Fitzgerald I can possible imagine)—myself still hobbling past the tennis courts where the lively and the lucky and the imperishably graceful play at their beautiful bloodless game. And where I was once gnawed with envy I am now stunned with simple admiration. For I myself seem to have aged into that second childhood where indifference becomes a sort of mimic innocence and even justice seems irrelevant.

And here to conclude things for me is an even older man—one who outlived Raleigh by many years—Sir Robert Carey, first cousin to Queen Elizabeth, a soldier, a gambler and a seafaring man who, among other things, brought the word to the young King James that the old Queen was dead and gone and that he, James, was now to be King of England, France, and Ireland, Defender of the Faith, etc.

Carey, more given to action than contemplation, wrote the only genuine autobiography we have from that time. He had just been named Earl of Monmouth in 1626. And here he is, in *The Succession*, as he wakes on the day of that year on which he will begin to write that memoir, composing a passage that ends with the first words of it: "*Now they are beginning to vanish. As if stepping backwards into shadows and stealing away from me. Slowly and surely. Whose face can that be?*" The Earl says this to himself. Not aloud. Merely mouthing words, tasting them. They seem to describe something he was dreaming only a moment or two before, though what he was dreaming he cannot remember. He has awakened to find himself saying these words without making a sound. Well, why not? There is no one for him to say them to in his bedchamber. No one else here except a young servant boy asleep on a pallet in the dark corner nearest the chamber door. Boy groans something wordless from the deep place of his own dreaming. And then begins to snore.

The moon has long since passed over. And gone down. Could it be any darker in a tomb? He doubts it. And now he thinks he understands why those old pharoahs of Egypt and other heathen and pagan kings and emperors wanted to have their servants buried with them. In a tomb, in the dark of his own grave, the Earl would find the groans and snores of the oaf to be deeply reassuring. As they reassure him even now. He smiles to himself, trying to imagine the look on that lout's face if he was told that he was about to be entombed with the Earl.

There. Again. Another face. Angry and startled. Whose? What is it?

Soon the last darkness will begin to thin out. Will slowly become gray. Then gray will begin to change until there is the softest hint of rose and pink at the window. Next the cock of the kitchen garden will crow his first doodledoo. Birds in the trees of park and garden will tune and sing. Closer, just beyond the window, he will hear the soft, repetitive, four-note flute sounds of a mourning dove.

Then suddenly all the trumpets of the rising sun.

Well, sun seldom if ever finds him asleep enough to be startled by its arrival. For he sleeps little. Never has.

When he did doze, eased into sleep awhile ago, there were still some patches of gold, faint tatters of moonlight in the chamber. And the servant, asleep or not, made not a noise. Earl lay still, curtained and softly floating in his four-poster bed. Thinking that he had heard the sound of an owl. Believing that if he lay there, keeping himself very quiet and very still, breathing ever so lightly, he might hear that owl again. Some men fear the owl as the messenger of death and disasters. Well, he has listened for and heard owls for fifty years and still death has not come scratching at his door. Not yet. Meantime, the hoot of an owl can be a great comfort to an old man half-awake and with nobody to talk to.

So he lay there content, waiting for the sound. And feeling the smooth, warm, clean texture of the linen sheets, all freshly washed and sunned and aired in this fine weather. Sheets not so fine as were Leicester's, each with his crest and initials embroidered in its corner. But those are gone to rags or to feed moths now, together with the dozens of damask table cloths he kept in this castle. Well, these are fine enough and clean enough to please a man who once and often slept on cold ground with only wide sky and stars for his covering.

He has not yet permitted himself the luxury of forgetting how that was.

He felt the linen sheets he was lapped in. And breathed the scent of lavender from sheets and pillows. Which scent he prefers to the saffron that so many folks use. And, feeling himself to be ageless and bodiless, without an ache or pain to his name, he waited for the owl to call again. And so he . . . fell asleep. Into that dream from which he just now returned. Out of which he was speaking intently to someone. Most likely talking to himself.

There was, though, that face. Remembers that. Indeed can now see it in his mind's eye—a thin, pinched, scarred, crow-trodden, blue-eyed face. Fairhaired, too, but wearing a bloody bandage on his head. But whose? Who is it? Cannot remember. . . .

Well, he could sleep again if he chose to. If he would close his eyes again, breathe in the sweet scent of lavender . . . which, if it can, as they say, calm and tame a ferocious lion, then why not also an aged and irrascible earl?

Could, but he will not. Instead, will stare into the dark and listen for any sounds. And wait for the rising of the sun. Because he has rested enough. Because he can think of nothing else that he is eager to dream of. And, no denying it, because something or other in the dream he was just set free from has left him vaguely troubled and uneasy.

All yesterday was a fine day. Early he was on horseback. In the heat of the morning, before dinnertime, he and the young scholar walked and talked in the garden. Which is much improved already. And now they have been able to repair the pipes and to make that fountain of Leicester's begin its dance again. After a fashion. Heat of the day, but he and his companion stood and talked in the cool mist of the playing fountain. About this and that. About everything. How it was. How it has been. How it may be. Continued until they were invited in to table. And after dinner with their wine and cheese and fruit and nuts. Until it was time to rest himself a little.

Then, after his napping, he went with some of the others out to the shady green, shadowed from sun by the walls, where they could play at bowling. And where the earl, who has not yet lost his skill at it, made some wagers. And won money from them.

Supper was excellent. Ate lightly, but still had his fill of a good fresh green sallet with herbs, a poached pigeon cooked with berries and fruit, and a fat capon prepared with a sauce of wine and oranges. Finished it with a cold Italian cream and some almond tarts. Washed down by the best and sweetest malmsey he has tasted in some time.

Everything was so well, so delicately cooked that he cannot blame his dream on bad digestion. Which he would not admit to in any case. Lest he should be persuaded of the need for purging. Which he is sure would kill him. These doctors with their purges will kill a man long before his time.

When he dies, let it not be from medicine. Let it rather be from an excess of malmsey, a surfeit of cold Italian cream.

Wonders if Leicester served his guests that dish. And if they found the courage to eat it at his table. No doubt it was worth a poisoning.

Can picture the sudden surprise on a blank face, an imaginary someone or other who has only just surmised that his sweet, cold Italian cream is deadly, is the last sweet thing he will ever eat. . . .

There now. That face again. Face from the dream returns now. Eyes bulged and popping with surprise and outrage and something more. Eyes clouded with sudden and shadowy knowledge of death. Not death by poison. Not the look of a man who has been sliced or carved with sharp steel. No. This fellow is hanging by the neck. Strangling. Going blue and black in the face.

But it is not the hanging that so astonishes and angers him. He was born to hang and knows it. Knew it. Only serious question was when. And where. And by whom.

No. It is more. Pure and angry astonishment of a man who has been badly tricked. And all of a sudden, at one moment (which happens to be his last), knows it.

Very satisfactory for the trickster.

Ah, well.

And now it comes clear whose face was troubling his dream.

Fellow by name of Geordie Bourne. Who else? Scotsman and a thief from birth and a great reiver of the East March.

Taken by some of Carey's men in a bloody little fight. Geordie fought bravely as always. But in a poor place and there were, for once, too many of them for him.

Close friend to Sir Robert Ker, this Geordie was. Who sent word to Carey how he would do a great deal and be willing to give much to save Geordie's hide. And how (also) if means were not found to save his life, why then Ker would bring fire and sword and utter destruction to the English side.

We shall see about that.

His aim at that time was to make mischief for Robert Ker. To teach him
something. To shame him. To catch him if he could. So he called a jury.
Which promptly found Geordie guilty of March-Treason. And sentenced
him to death.

Then waited to see what Ker might do. Whether to hang the fellow or
not.

Determined to go and see the fellow with his own eyes. For he and
Geordie had not yet met or seen each other face to face.

Here is how the Earl will write about it in his memoirs:

When all things were quiet and the watch set at night, after supper about ten of the
clock, I took one of my men's liveries and put it about me. And took two other of my
servants with me in their liveries. And we three, as the Warden's men, came to
where Bourne was kept and were let into his chamber. We sat down by him and
told him that we were desirous to see him because we had heard he was stout
and valiant and true to his friend. And that we were sorry that our master could not
be moved to save his life.

Then they talked awhile. And Geordie, a true reiver to the bones,
could not help himself from telling them the story of his life.

"Told us that he had lain with at least forty men's wives, some in England, some in Scotland. That he had killed seven Englishmen with his
own hands. And that he had spent his whole lifetime in whoring, drinking,
stealing and taking deep revenge for slight offenses."

Geordie asked them if they could send him a minister of the Gospel to
comfort his soul. Not that he was in great fear and trembling. But just in
case that Ker could not free him and it really came to a hanging.

"I was so resolved that no conditions should save his life. And so I
took order that at the opening of the gates on the next morning he should
be carried to execution. Which accordingly was performed. . . ."

Came there myself on my own horse to witness the hanging. Which
was what caused that memorable look to take command of Geordie's
face. Outrage, fury that he had been tricked into confessing (or brag-
ging, if you prefer) his lifetime of sins and crimes. Not to three common
and simpleminded Englishmen, as it seemed. But to the very Warden,
himself. To whom so many (and especially Ker) on both sides of the
Border were busily making representation of the excellent character and
reputation of the aforesaid selfsame Geordie Bourne and of all the rea-

sons why such a man of good Christian character and decent repute should be spared.

Oh, it took considerable effort not to laugh out loud at the moment when their eyes met and Geordie Bourne recognized him. And showed that he did with the last living expression of his face.

Lord, that would have been ill-mannered and unseemly, to laugh in the face of a man you have condemned and hanged.

God's death, the fellow was deeply surprised, though, was he not? About as much as a man can be. Though only briefly.

So was Ker surprised. And even more angry. Well . . . he had time to cultivate his anger. I never knew a man to be so angry about anything as Ker was. You would think he honestly believed that Geordie Bourne would die with his boots off in bed.

In the end, though, Ker and I were friends. After a fashion. It took some time and some doing, but we finally shook hands on it and even drank to the memory of Geordie Bourne.

Another story. And another story he cannot tell his young Oxford scholar. Who, in his youth and high seriousness, will not be able to understand the lighthearted spirit of it. Best not to mention that one. Best to write it down and be done with it. Else Geordie may continue to come into his dreams. And others, too.

Lord, if half the men he has had to hang (for their own good and the good of the Borders) return to people his dreams, his nights will be more crowded with faces than the Court at Christmas. And such ugly faces. Wonderful, rough, and everlastingly ugly faces. . . .

He thinks it might be rude and unseemly even now to laugh out loud in the privacy of his own bed chamber. Yet he cannot suppress it any more.

And his laughter fills the room. Startles the servant awake.

And so begins another summer's day.

Well, the trick has turned on him now. He can delay and procrastinate no longer.

Time has come to tune or play the lute. To write it down and forget about it.

Pens sharpened. Inkhorn and paper and plenty of fine sand for plenty of blotting.

No more excuses or diversions.

George Garrett

Robert Carey, Baron of Leppington, and Earl of Monmouth, must and will begin to write his memories.

He will begin, as is the oldest custom, with a prayer:

"Oh Lord, my God, open mine eyes and enlarge my heart with a true understanding of Thy great mercies, that Thou has blessed me withal, from my first being until this my old age. And give me of Thy grace to call in mind some measure of Thy great and manifold blessings that Thou hast blessed me withal. Though my weakness be such and my memory so short, as I have not abilities to express them as I ought to do, yet, Lord, be pleased to accept of this sacrifice of praise and thanksgiving. . . ."

John Irving

The Narrative Voice

Whenever writers gather, or when there's a gathering around just one writer, it is wise to remember the very little worth of Oscar Wilde—whose actual literature will hardly be remembered, at all, one day, but whose witty one-liners (especially about his superiors—Dickens and Flaubert, for example) will unfortunately linger with us for a while longer. One-liners deserve to be short-lived, but they are easier to remember than more complicated things—than actual literature, for example—and they're useful during speeches, and at parties.

Wilde once remarked that Flaubert's conversation was on a level with the conversation of a pork-butcher. A funny thing to say, but what does it reveal? It tells us that Flaubert was not in the conversation business, I guess; it suggests that Wilde's major enterprise was conversation—or that, at least, in the presence of a larger writer than himself, Wilde was reduced to the cattiness of a gossip columnist. Of course, alongside Flaubert's literature, the work of Wilde is on the level of butchery. Of writing itself, for example, Flaubert has written: "Human language is a cracked kettle, on which we beat our tunes for bears to dance to, when all the while we wish to move the stars to pity." Fancy a pork-butcher saying that? Fancy Oscar Wilde risking "pity."

This makes a strong impression on me: what is always established in a great writer's voice is pity, is sympathy—in the case of the Flaubert statement, sympathy for the necessary struggle with language, which is every writer's struggle. What is always established in a minor writer's voice is bitchiness. And what a minor writer most relishes criticizing in a major writer's work are what Flaubert called those ever-awkward "tunes for bears to dance to"; the attempt to "move the stars to pity" is least understood by the minor writer, and easiest to attack.

Sentiment is always vulnerable; when the fictional voice deliberately seeks to move you, it is an unguarded and completely exposed voice. It is easy to feel intellectually superior to such a voice. It is easy to assume that a book is a creation of and for the *mind*. And was it ever in good taste (intellectually) to encourage emotional responses—or worse, to be guided through a book by emotional responses? But a great writer guides you from one emotional response to another; a great writer isn't careful (he's not worried about offending your good taste). Good taste is too tidy a position for him. Good taste is too contained—a cramped backyard, where your own pets and children are temporarily restrained, or kept safe; where other people's pets and children are prevented entry. Good taste is the suburbs of literature! There have been some rare and great writers who've managed life (and work) in the suburbs—who've managed to be "in good taste"—but it is not where most great writers work (some do manage to live there, without damage).

I believe that a novel works more magic upon a reader by moving the reader emotionally than by convincing the reader intellectually—although, of course, these pleasures needn't be exclusive. I believe that the voice of a novel isn't really educational; it may be (to some) enlightening, it may nurture the spirit. I admit that I'm more interested in speaking to the spirit than to the mind. I believe in what a character in a Robertson Davies novel expresses, rather ruthlessly, when he says: "If . . . education has any bearing on the arts at all, its purpose is to make critics, not artists. Its usual effect is to cage the spirit in other people's ideas—the ideas of poets and philosophers, which were once splendid insights into the nature of life, but which people who have no insights of their own have hardened into dogmas. It is the spirit we must work with, and not the mind as such."

I hope none of you turns what I say into dogma, or misunderstands me to the extent that you suppose *I* am speaking dogma. Of course, I will admit to holding certain priorities in the novel higher than others. I also admit that a novel is a house of many mansions—the form is generous, and may be celebrated in a variety of voices. It's no secret to anyone who's read me that the voice I love best is the narrative voice, is the storyteller's voice. I believe that narrative momentum must override description, must restrain all our pretty abilities with the language, must be more strongly felt than even necessary information—especially technical information—which, although it is necessary for authenticity in any narrative, must never dominate or make secondary the *story*. The only thing (in my opinion) that narrative momentum must not override is character—for the building and the development of characters, even narrative must pause and wait its turn.

The forward motion of a good story, the drive of linear narration—of several linear narratives if you prefer—and developed characters: these may strike you as old-fashioned priorities in the novel, but the great novels of the nineteenth century are still the models of the form for me.

The narrative voice has to work hardest at the beginning—at every beginning, because in any novel there are many beginnings. At the start of any story, at the introduction of any character, the narrative voice must take a firm grip on the reader and not let the reader's attention wander; the voice, in the beginning, is full of promises—full of bluffing, full of threatening, full of hints. What the voice seeks to establish is a situation in which the possibilities for good stories are rich; the voice also needs to establish a character, or characters, to whom good stories can happen—people who seem vulnerable enough to have big things happen to them, yet sturdy enough to withstand the bad news ahead. What I always try to hear in the narrative voice is the sound of a potential myth, a possible legend.

One method of the narrative voice, in the beginning, is to adopt the voice of telling a very *old* story, a story that was always there; and the voice, patiently, in its own good time, will get to the good stuff—that's a promise—but you're going to have to *wait*.

Chapter One of *The Cider House Rules* begins:

In the hospital of the orphanage—the boys' division at St. Cloud's, Maine—two nurses were in charge of naming the new babies and checking that their little penises were healing (from the obligatory circumcision).

The narrative voice has (I hope you will hear) a tone of legend. In this respect, the beginning of Chapter Two is similar to that of Chapter One.

A child of Maine, Wilbur Larch was born in Portland in 186_ —the son of a sullen, tidy woman who was among the staff of cooks and housekeepers for a man named Neal Dow, the Mayor of Portland and the so-called father of the Maine law which introduced prohibition to that state. Neal Dow once ran for the Presidency as the candidate of the Prohibition Party, but he won barely ten thousand votes— proving that the general voter was wiser than Wilbur Larch's mother, who worshipped her employer and saw herself more as his co-worker for temperance reform than as his servant (which she was).

Interestingly, Wilbur Larch's father was a drunk—no small feat in the Portland of Mayor Dow's day.

When a story has developed, and—as importantly—its characters have been developed, one can afford a flat, matter-of-fact tone to the narrative (a less dense, less parenthetical style). Just the mention of a character's name is enough (for instance, the name of Melony, who at the beginning of Chapter Seven is a sullen thug, hunting the main character down). But even the beginning of a late chapter in a novel must still sound like a beginning—perhaps to a story within the larger story.

One day that August a hazy sun hung over the coastal road between York Harbor and Ogonquit; it was not the staring sun of Marseilles, and not the cool, crisp sun that blinks on much of the coast of Maine at that time of year. It was a St. Cloud's sunlight, steamy and flat, and Melony was irritated by it, and sweating, when she accepted a ride in a milk truck that was heading inland.

The other, most distinctive voice that narrative employs is the voice of summary, the concluding voice—the voice that ends things. I think that every chapter ending somehow should foreshadow the end of the novel itself—which should have in its final voice the echoes of all the other endings we've heard.

Here is the sound of the end of Chapter Eight:

"Shot down!" Candy was screaming, when Homer finally shut off the ignition. "He was shot down—over Burma!"

"Over Burma," said Homer Wells. He dismounted from the tractor and held the sobbing girl in his arms; although the tractor was shut-off, the engine still knocked, and then shuddered, and then throbbed. The engine gave off those little prickly sounds and its heat made the air shimmer. Maybe, thought Homer Wells, the air is always shimmering over Burma.

The end of Chapter Nine is similar in tone:

"I awoke without having parted in my sleep with the perception of my wretchedness," Wilbur Larch had read aloud. Either Dr. Larch had pre-determined that he
would end the evening's reading with that line, or else he had only then noticed
Candy and Homer Wells in the open doorway—the harsh hall light, a naked bulb,
formed a kind of institutional halo above their heads—and Larch had lost his
place in the book and therefore, spur-of-the-moment, he had stopped reading.
For whatever reason, that perception of wretchedness had been Candy's introduction to St. Cloud's, and the beginning and the end of her bedtime story.

The passage with which Dr. Larch concludes his reading is from
Great Expectations, which itself contains (in some editions) the *two* mar-
velous endings (and ending voices) that Dickens wrote to that novel.
Much has been written about how modern, and better, the original ending (which Dickens abandoned) is—and how simply romantic and sentimental his revised ending was. I prefer the one he finally chose. What
interests me is how similar the voices are: there is a great difference
between the voice of unrequited love (and self-pity) and the voice of a
happy ending, but there is most of all melancholy and nostalgia in both
voices.

The original ending follows:

I was very glad afterwards to have had the interview, for in her [Estella's] face and
in her voice, and in her touch, she gave me the assurance that suffering had been
stronger than Miss Havisham's teaching, and had given her a heart to understand
what my heart used to be.

And the revised:

I took her hand in mine, and we went out of the ruined place; and as the morning
mists had risen long ago when I first left the forge, so the evening mists were rising
now, and in all the broad expanse of tranquil light they showed to me, I saw no
shadow of another parting from her.

There are many endings in a final chapter of any strongly narrative
novel. The voice of summary is ever-present in the vicinity of the actual
ending—even in the simplest, descriptive passages.

Even the word *end* appears frequently, and naturally enough. This
passage is less than twenty manuscript pages from the actual ending of
The Cider House Rules:

At the end of the harvest, on a gray morning with a wild wind blowing in from the ocean, the overhead bulb that hung in the cider house kitchen blinked twice and burned out; the spatter of apple-mash on the far wall, near the press and grinder, was cast so somberly in shadows that the dark clots of pomace looked like black leaves that had blown indoors and stuck against the wall in a storm.

Lastly, there is even a beginning voice to one's ending: that is, there is the beginning of the ending. It is the moment when the future is suggested, when an epilogue can be heard, often indicated as simply as by the tense of the verb (in this case, *would*). Here is the beginning of the ending to *The Cider House Rules*. It is still narrative in tone, only now it is projecting something (into the future); it is still a storytelling, not a preaching, voice.

It is the word *would* that announces the future (and the voice that will speak the ending of the novel—only five manuscript pages away from this passage).

In the constantly changing weather of Maine, and most especially on cloudy days, the presence of St. Cloud's could be felt in Heart's Rock; with a heavy certainty, the air of St. Cloud's could be distinguished in the trapped stillness that hovered above the water of Drinkwater Lake (like those water bugs, those water walkers, that were nearly constant there). And even in the fog that rolled over those bright, coastal lawns of Heart's Haven's well-to-do, there was sometimes in the storm-coming air that leaden, heart-sinking feeling that was the essence of the air of St. Cloud's. So that even after he had left them, Candy and Wally and Angel would think about Homer Wells.

At the end of every good story, there is the suggestion of the idea about how to live a new life.

Lee Smith

■■■■■■■■■■■■■■

■■■■
The Voice behind the Story

When I first began writing in my college days, nothing I wrote was very good. I was taking the introductory creative writing course at Hollins College, and my average was a *B−*. Sometimes I got a *C+*.

The problem was that I thought I had to think up something exciting, something glamorous, to write about. One of my early main characters, I remember, was a stewardess in Hawaii named Cecile. Or occasionally I came up with a story strong in theme—which, in my case, meant sappy and melodramatic. I am reminded of my story about the whole family that died in a fire on Christmas Eve and when the rescue squad arrived, the only thing left intact was a little music box among the ashes playing "Silent Night." *C−* for that one.

My teachers kept telling me, "Write what you know," but I didn't know, for a long time, what that was.

Then, in Louis Rubin's southern literature class, I came upon the stories of Eudora Welty and Flannery O'Connor. It was as though a literal light bulb snapped on in my head, exactly the way it happens in cartoons, because I realized that these writers hadn't been anywhere I hadn't been, and didn't know anybody I didn't know. Now that was arrogant, but when you're eighteen years old you *are* arrogant, and anyway it didn't matter. For the first time I began to have a sense of what I knew, of what my subject might be. I remembered a man in Grundy, up in the mountains where I'm from, telling me how, if you buy a woman a set of new teeth, she'll leave you every time. I remembered ladies sitting on the front porch engaged in endless discussions about whether somebody did or did not have colitis. I began to think I might have something to say. Something about families, and about daily life, and small towns, and kids, and about expectations and reality and that point where they collide, because that's the point—I realized this much later—where the story happens.

I've heard Max Steele say that nothing is ever finally fiction. If it didn't happen to us, he says, then it might have, or it might have happened to a friend of ours, or at least it *should* have, or maybe it happened to us in some other life, or it might as well have. I think this is true. Every event we think we make up corresponds to an emotional reality, or to a psychological reality, or to an experience we have dreamed.

I am reminded of Anne Tyler, who once said, "I write because I want to have more than one life." This is the point: it's ALL US, finally, in some awful and wonderful way. The trick is to find a means to handle the material so that it will be true and meaningful for us, yet in such a way that we can feel free to juggle the facts and conditions in order to achieve the maximum aesthetic effect.

Real life, of course, is chaos. Cause and effect are crazy. Often it all seems entirely whimsical, or tragic, or ridiculous—at best, arbitrary. What the writer does is impose an order on all this chaos. That's what plot is about. But to do this most effectively, this drawing order out of chaos, we have to be neither too close to nor too far from our chosen—or given—material.

This appropriate distance can best be achieved, I think, through choosing the right point of view for any given story. If I want to write a story based on something that really happened to me, for instance, I will usually put it in the third person point of view and change the character radically so I can feel free enough of it to maintain aesthetic control. But all writers have to figure out for themselves how to manipulate point of view in their own best interests. In any case, here are a few things to consider in choosing the angle of narration.

By using the first-person point of view, with a reliable narrator, a very special kind of closeness can be achieved almost immediately with the reader. The main character is easily developed because he or she is speaking, and it's easy to control plot—you can only tell whatever the main character sees or thinks or hears. On the negative side, this can be severely limiting. But first person is not restricted to the reliable narrator; we can have an unreliable narrator, too, like Sister in "Why I Live at the P.O." The unreliable speaker often reveals things to the reader of which he or she is unaware, adding a whole level of complexity to the story. This makes the reader work harder, and the reader loves to work.

Or we can have a first-person narrator who is telling a story about somebody else. Good examples are John Cheever's story "Torch Song" and Melville's "Bartleby the Scrivener." This is a tricky point of view in one respect because, at the end, the inevitable question comes up: exactly why has this narrator told us this story? What does it mean to the narrator? And we have to deal with that.

If we use the close third-person point of view, we can have the main advantage of the first-person narrator—open access to one character's consciousness—with the added advantage of being able to tell many things about our main character which he would not tell about himself. What he's wearing, for instance, or how he walks across a room.

The other option is the omniscient—the most flexible, the most unrestricted and the hardest, finally, for me, because it offers too many options.

But the writer's voice is really what we're talking about here. Having found the subject and the point of view necessary to distance the material, the writer has already gone a long way toward finding a voice. Because the writer's voice will always be heard. Sometimes the whole process of contemporary literature seems to me to be a voyage into narcissism: in, in, down further and further into consciousness, with the writer intruding more and more into the work. The writer has become less concerned with the grand design, with the whole of society, and has become more and more focused upon the individual consciousness, and upon himself. This is partly because our real world has become so fragmented and diffuse and confusing that we feel we can't attempt to see it whole and partly because we have moved, it seems to me, farther away from our old beliefs and closer to the contemplation of our own psyches as the ultimate reality. This trend reached a kind of apogee, I think, with the publication of D. M. Thomas's extraordinary novel *The White Hotel,* in which Thomas attempts to set up Freudian analysis as the sustaining myth of our time.

In any case, the writer will be heard. Let's explore that for a second.

What is the "voice" I'm talking about? How is it established? From what does it derive? First, from exactly that idea of *subject* I mentioned earlier. What does a writer write *about*? What is the world of the fiction? What kind of people typically inhabit it? When I think of Walker Percy, for instance, a visual image immediately springs to mind: it is a large, well-kept southern golf course, with pine trees in the rough and exceptional water hazards. This is his fictional terrain, just as John Cheever inhabited upper-class suburbia and John Updike inhabits any house in any middle-class neighborhood. Here, for an example, is what I'm talking about, the Third World milieu of V. S. Naipaul, at the beginning of *Guerillas*:

The sea smelled of swamp; it barely rippled, had glitter rather than color; and the heat seemed trapped below the pink haze of bauxite dust from the bauxite loading station. After the market, where refrigerated trailers were unloading; after the rubbish dump burning in the remnant of mangrove swamp, with black carrion corbeaux squatting hunched on fence posts or hopping about on the ground; after the built-up hillsides; after the new housing estates, rows of unpainted boxes of concrete and corrugated iron already returning to the shantytowns that had been knocked down for this development; after the naked children playing in the red dust of the straight new avenues, the clothes hanging like rags from back yard lines; after this, the land cleared a little. And it was possible to see over what the city had spread: on one side, the swamp, drying out to a great plain; on the side, a chain of hills, rising directly from the plain.

The openness didn't last for long. Villages had become suburbs. Sometimes the side wall of a concrete house was painted over with an advertisement. In the fields that had survived there were billboards. And soon there was a factory area. It was here that the signs for Thrushcross Grange began: the name, the distance in miles, a clenched fist emblematically rendered, the slogan For the Land and for the Revolution, and in a strip at the bottom the name of the firm that had put the sign up. The signs were all new. The local bottlers of Coca-Cola had put one up; so had the American Bauxite Co., a number of airlines, and many stores in the city.

Jane said, "Jimmy's frightened a lot of people."

So we have the writer's fictional terrain to consider, and often we have a particular kind of character who turns up again and again because he's at home there. Here are two paragraphs from the beginning of Raymond Carver's story, "Mr. Coffee and Mr. Fixit." Carver frequently uses first-person narrators.

I've seen some things. I was going over to my mother's to stay a few nights. But just as I got to the top of the stairs, I looked and she was on the sofa kissing a man. It was summer. The door was open. The TV was going. That's one of the things I've seen.

My mother is sixty-five. She belongs to a singles club. Even so, it was hard. I stood with my hand on the railing and watched as the man kissed her. She was kissing him back, and the TV was going.

Carver characters are somewhat similar to Barry Hannah's characters, except that Hannah is wackier and darker. Here's the narrator of Hannah's story "Love Too Long," telling us about himself:

My head's burning off and I got a heart about to bust out of my ribs. All I can do is move from chair to chair with my cigarette. I wear shades. I can't read a magazine. Some days I take my binoculars and look out in the air. They laid me off. I can't find work. My wife's got a job and she takes flying lessons. When she comes over the house in her airplane, I'm afraid she'll screw up and crash.

I got to get back to work and get dulled out again. I got to be a man again. You can't walk around the house drinking coffee and beer all day, thinking about her taking her brassiere off. We been married and divorced twice. Sometimes I wish I had a sport. I bought a croquet set on credit at Penny's. First day I got so tired of it I knocked the balls off in the weeds and they're out there rotting, mildew all over them, I bet, but I don't want to see.

After the place and the people, we come inevitably to the question of *tone:* what attitude is the writer taking toward this material. Is it ironic? Are we meant to believe it? or what? Sometimes this is easy, as when we pick up a story by Donald Barthelme and begin to read about angels.

But sometimes the question is more complicated, as in *The French Lieutenant's Woman,* when the intrusive narrative voice continually reminds us that there is a writer manipulating these characters: and forcing us finally to choose the ending. Are we to believe, or not believe? We are meant, I think, to do something rather more complex, just as we are meant to respond to certain South American writers—as we are meant to respond to Tim O'Brien's novel *Searching for Cacciato,* in which the author sets up, in effect, alternate—yet equally believable—realities.

Of course, ambivalence of tone is not new to American writing, but goes way back to the writer's search for an American language that might combine all the old eloquence, all the grand themes, of English literature with the raw new vernacular of our country and with the kind of people who have lived here. Nothing, especially tone, is ever separate from *language,* either, and we can trace this combination of the high-falutin' and the mundane back to Twain, to Whitman, and especially to William Faulkner. I would like to cite a brief section from *As I Lay Dying.* This is Darl's point of view.

"If you see a good-sized can, you might bring it," I say. Dewey Dell gets down from the wagon, carrying the package. "You had more trouble than you expected, selling these cakes in Mottson," I say. How do our lives ravel out into the no-wind, no-sound, the weary gestures wearily recapitulant; echoes of old compulsions with no-hand on no-strings: in sunset we fall into furious attitudes, dead gestures of dolls. Cash broke his leg and now the sawdust is running out. He is bleeding to death is Cash.

"I wouldn't be beholden," pa says. "God knows."

So we frequently find, in contemporary writing, an ambiguity of tone, a blend of realism with surrealism or hyperbole, and often a return to mythic elements. Here's the end of Eudora Welty's story "The Wanderers." An old beggar woman has just sat down next to Virgie Rainey on the stile.

Occasional drops of rain fell on Virgie's hair on her cheek, or rolled down her arm, like a cool finger; only it was not, as if it had never been, a finger, being the rain out of the sky. October rain on Mississippi fields. The rain of fall, maybe on the whole South, for all she knew on the everywhere. She stared into its magnitude.

She smiled once, seeing before her, screenlike, the hideous and delectable face Mr. King McClain had made at the funeral, and when they all knew he was next, even he. Then she and the old beggar woman, the old black thief, were there alone and together in the shelter of the big public tree, listening to the magical percussion, the world beating in their ears. They heard through falling rain the running of the horse and bear, the stroke of the leopard, the dragon's crusty slither, and the glimmer and the trumpet of the swan.

Thinking about Eudora Welty reminds me of how crucial these points of style become for those of us who are from the South, and who are writing about the South. We don't have any new material. We all have doomed cousins who are still going to Sweetbriar and crazy uncles who still live in their mothers' back rooms. A lot of the land is the same. Maybe we don't have the degree of racial guilt, but there's always plenty of general southern guilt to go around. So what are we going to do? How are we going to write about what we know, yet keep it from being trite—keep it from being a bad imitation of those writers we most admire, Faulkner and Eudora Welty and Flannery O'Connor, all those people who have "done" southern so well?

The best we can hope for, since we can't just wish away all those givens we have to work with, is to make it new *through language*—through point of view, through tone, through style. And this is happening all over the place. Bobbie Ann Mason throws all the hyperbole out the window and deals with her people—people who drive school buses and who say Datsun dog, for instance—with a clear, direct, unsentimental precision. It would be so easy to romanticize her people, yet she never does. Walker Percy's ironic detachment; Cormac McCarthy's lush yet enigmatic fables; the way Barry Hannah uses all the old Southern elements but stands them on their heads; Breece Pancake's dark vision; Anne Tyler's abiding sense of magic and the deep mystery at the heart of family life—all these are stylistic approaches, really, to making it brand new.

Even the small considerations of language contribute to any writer's voice: such prosaic questions as the length of the sentences, the favored grammatical constructions, the imagery, or the lack of imagery. All these are points of style, and it is only through style finally—through language—that any writer can be original. All the themes are old.

So we come to the quality of the prose. Is it lean, spare, and reductive, like, say the work of Joan Didion or Grace Paley? Is it lush, full, almost overblown, like that of Joyce Carol Oates? What degree of development is given? How much detail is given, and what kind of detail? Ann Beattie, for instance, rarely gives a physical description of any of her characters. Many contemporary writers write in the present tense and avoid referring to the past at all in the way in which we have traditionally used it, to illuminate character in the present moment of the story.

And a final thought in determining any writer's voice: how present is the author in the work?

Although I had been writing for a long time, I had never, it seemed to me, been able to deal with some of my best material—mostly, the things having to do with my growing up in the mountains. I couldn't write it straight, was the problem. I still felt all the old ambivalence you feel about the place you grew up in. So one day I was kind of messing around, and I wrote the beginning of a story:

Geneva moves through a dream these days. Right now she sits in a straightback kitchen chair on the front porch, stringing pole beans on a newspaper on her lap and looking up every now and then at the falling-down sidetrack up on the mountain across the road, at the dusty green leaves the way they curl up in the heat, at nothing. It is real hot. The black hair on Geneva's forehead sticks to her skin and she keeps on pushing it back. She strings the beans and breaks them in two and drops them into the pot by her side without once looking down. She feels a change coming on. Geneva has known that something is up ever since last Wednesday night when she hollered out in church.

As soon as I wrote that, I felt the most enormous sense of relief. All of a sudden I was using the way the characters spoke *in the narrative voice,* which plenty of other writers have done, but which had never really occurred to me. This sounds minor, perhaps, but it freed me up enormously. Now I felt that I could write about my characters without writing down to them, because I was using their words, but I wasn't restricted to their words, either. I was using what Tom Wolfe has called the *downstage narrative voice.* All the ambivalence I felt could be contained stylistically. It would even be part of the story, so I could tell what I wanted to tell. Suddenly I could tell things—revivals and beauty contests and first dates and 4-H potato salad-making contests—which I had not been able to tell before.

Since then I've become more and more intrusive, and the writing has come more and more easily. In a short story named "Cakewalk," for instance, I amazed myself by breaking into the narrative with this comment straight from me, the writer—there is not really any narrator in this story.

There comes a time in a woman's life when the children take over, and what you do is what you have to, and it seems like the days go by so slow while you're home with them, and nothing ever really gets done around the house before you have to go off and do something else which doesn't ever get done either, and it can take you all day long to hem a skirt. Every day lasts a long, long time. But then before you know it, it's all over, those days gone like a fog on the mountain, and the kids are all in school and there you are with this awful light empty feeling in your stomach like the beginning of cramps, when you sit in the chair where you used to nurse the baby and listen to the radio news.

I can't say whether it's good or bad that I have fallen upon this kind of an intrusive, down-home narrative voice. I don't even know that it works. But it has made it possible for me to write about what I want to write about right now—the people I'm interested in, their lives and times.

William Gass

■■■■■■■■■■■■■■■■■■

■■■■■
And

is used 3381 times in James Joyce's *A Portrait of the Artist as a Young Man*, and occurs in 7170 occasions in that same author's *Ulysses*, from which we can conclude that the latter is a much longer book. It appears oftener than *a* and oftener than *an*—although its frequency lags far behind *the* (as regards ubiquity always the winner)—and it easily outdoes *or, of, it, oh*, as well as every other little word that might be presumed to be its rival, even *is*, even *1*.[1] Of the number of words we use in ordinary correspondence, *I, the*, and *and*, at one time at least, made up an impressive eighth, whereas in telephone conversations, some snoop has reported,[2] *and* barely makes the top ten.

Words that get heavy, one might say almost continuous, employment are invariably short. Suppose *and* were as long as *moreover*? It would soon *mean* "moreover," and drop to an ignominious rate of three in *A Portrait*, to a sad two in *Ulysses*, a frequency that will scarcely seed a satisfying life. And if *and* were spelled, say, like *Mesopotamia*, would it receive any use at all? And what would happen to the ideas it represents,

1. *Word Index to James Joyce's Portrait of the Artist*, comp. by Leslie Hancock (Carbondale, Ill.: Southern Illinois University Press, 1967) and *Word Index to James Joyce's Ulysses*, comp. by Miles L. Hanley (Madison, Wisconsin, 1937).

2. The Bell System, of course. H. L. Mencken, *The American Language, Supplement Two*. (New York: Alfred Knopf, 1948), p. 352.

if we were too busy to think them, or to all the various ands in the world we could no longer trouble ourselves to designate? That ceaselessly constant conjunction of which Hume spoke would now be noted only rarely: when we were forced to remind ourselves of the connection between Punch moreover Judy, or Mutt mesopotamia Jeff.

Such is not its or our plight, however. On word lists, *and's* occurrences are merely numbered, never cited. The dictionary contains it only as a courtesy, and out of a traditional conceit for completeness. No one is going to look up *and.* We do not "look up" manhole covers when we visit the city. So it is a squeak we are used to. It passes through the ear, the eye, the mind, unheard, unseen, and unremarked. It can copulate as openly as birds do, the way park ducks wanton on their ponds. Indeed, pigeons are more heatedly complained of, for *and* leaves no poop on public shoulders. As a word, *and* is an amiable nothing. It hasn't even a substantiating, an ennobling function like *the,* which has caused many a philosopher's hackles to rise.

Joyce singled out *the* and gave it pride of final place in *Finnegans Wake,* although one might argue that while *the* has the last word in the body of the text, it acts only to buckle the belly of the book together, and that the pride of penultimate places is actually given to *a,* ordinarily a halt word, a rhyme chime, a mere space maker, the shallowest exhalation: *A way a lone a last a loved a long the* . . . where it interrupts the ells as they likker across the tongue: *lone lost loved long riverrun, past Eve and Adams, from swerve of shore to bend of bay* . . . *a* . . . *a* . . . *a.* . . . Just a few lines earlier, *and* had been allowed to perform an equally rocking rhythmical function: *And it's old and old it's sad and old it's sad and weary I go back to you, my cold father, my cold mad father, my cold mad feary father.* . . . It is worth noticing how *old* slips into an *O* like a woman into a wrapper: *And it's old and O it's sad and O it's sad and weary* . . . just as the *C* sound it picks up later will reinstruct our ears so that we hear, in retrospect, *And it's cold and cold it's sad and cold it's sad and weary.* . . . Of these musical methods, of course, Joyce was a master.

The anonymity of *and,* its very invisibility, recommends the word to the student of language, for when we really look at it, study it, listen to it, *and* no longer apears to be *and* at all, because *and* is, as we said, invisible, one of the threads that holds our clothes together: what business has it being a pant's leg or the frilly panel of a blouse? The unwatched word is meaningless—a noise in the nose—it falls on the page as it pleases, while the writer is worrying about nouns and verbs, welfare checks or a love affair; whereas the watched word has many meanings, some of them profound; it has a wide range of functions, some of them essential; it has many lessons to teach us about language, some of them surprising; and it has metaphysical significance of an even salutary sort.

And

is produced initially with an open mouth, the breath flowing out, but then that breath is driven up against the roof, toward the nose, even invading it before the sound is stoppered by the tongue against the teeth. The article *a* can be pronounced "aw," "A," "uh," "aah," or nearly forgotten, while *the* is "thuh" or "thee," depending on position and status; but *and* is only and always *and,* although its length, like many such words that contain the outrush of a vowel, is relatively indeterminate: "aah-nn-duh"—where the "duh" is like a lariat lassoing the next word, filling the voice stream, allowing one's thought to continue, inhibiting interruptions: "pahst Eeev AndunAahdummz. . . ." In Middle English, and often among the vulgar since, the word has appeared in reduced circumstances, either as a conditional: *an' it please your lordship, I'll drop me drawers*; or as a common conjunction: *an' here an' there the bullets went an' never touched me nearly.* Hollywood nosh nooks, back in the Thirties, bobbed it ever further: *Dunk 'n Dine,* their signs said, *Sit 'n Eat.* There was also the nautical *spit 'n polish,* and that enigmatic putdown *shit 'n shinola.*

Although the sound, "and," and the word, *and,* may appear and reappear in sentence after sentence, both in spoken and in written form, there is no single meaning (AND) that remains tethered to the token. The word is, perhaps, no sneakier than most words, but it is sneaky enough, hiding itself inside of other sounds, pulling syllables up over its head. It is, of course, the principal element in *randy, saraband,* and *island,* a not inconsiderable segment of *Andorra, Anderson, andeluvian, Spandau,* and *ampersand,* whose elegantly twisted symbol & (the so-called short or alphabetical *and* made by intertwining the *e* and *t* of *et*) also contains it. Since *ampersand* seems to be a slovenly corruption of the Latin laminated *and per se and,* which suggests an existence for itself as well as for others, a firm's name and book title like *Dombey and Son,* when written with the &, would mean "Dombey, both in his own person, and in the person of his son," a very forthright expression of the father's ownership. *And* also lurks about in words like *spanned,* and in apparently innocent commands like *please put the pan down, Anne,* as well as in many allegations or simple statements of fact, for instance, that *panders and pimps and pushers, panhandlers and prostitutes, stand like so many lamps on the streetcorners.*

Not only are there more *ands* about than immediately meets the eye, the word by itself in the open is manifold in its meanings, and not in the way that most words are ambiguous either: *bank* variously signifying a calculated bounce or guarded vault or sloping river edge; *rank* signifying something overripe or of military station; *tank* referring to an armored vehicle, a cylinder for gas or certain fluids, an approximate measure. *And* is ambiguous the way prepositions are, not straightforwardly but curvaciously, almost metaphysically, multiple. Think of the differences designated by the same, seemingly simple *on* in *the poorhouse is on fire, the seafood is on the table, her panties were hanging on the line, their lacy patterns turned him on, now his mind was mainly on Mary.*[3] Such words are constantly in transit between meanings, their very indeterminacy an invitation to their contexts to seize and to shape them; and if *bank* were like that, we should sense how we might slide down some weedy slope into the till, or how we might count on a good bounce from our rubber check.

Initially a preposition itself, and derived from *end,* the idea of fronting or facing a boundary, the word suggested an opposition, a standing of something next to but over against something else, such as *up* with *down, high* next to *low, peace* over against *war.* Later, as various words collapsed into and became *and (ond, ant, enti, anda, undi, und, unt, et,* etcetera), its function as a relatively neutral conjunction increased. Now not even Proteus can match the magicality of its many metamorphoses.

A single example from Gertrude Stein's "Melanctha" should be sufficient to show our small word's true and larger nature.

She tended Rose, and [#1] *she was patient, submissive, soothing, and* [#2] *untiring, while the sullen, childish, cowardly, black Rosie grumbled and* [#3] *fussed and* [#4] *howled and* [#5] *made herself to be an abomination and* [#6] *like a simple beast.*

3. I discuss the ambiguous character of the preposition *of,* citing fourteen different uses without presuming to have mentioned all of them, in "The Ontology of the Sentence, or How to Make a World of Words," *The World Within the Word* (New York: Alfred A. Knopf, 1978), pp. 308–38.

[*And* #1] *She tended Rose, and she was patient, submissive, soothing.* . . . This is the adverbial use of *and.* The expression is to be read: "She tended Rose, and (in doing so) she was patient, submissive, soothing. . . ." It is not so much that *and* is an adverb here; rather it determines the application of what follows it to the verb *tended.* We have no grammatical category for this operation.

[*And* #2] *she was patient, submissive, soothing, and untiring* . . . . This *and* begins as the *and* of balance and co-ordination. That is, we have *soothing* on the one hand balanced logically and grammatically with *untiring* like two weights on a scale. Both words belong to the same part of speech; both are about the same length; both designate qualities of the same logical order, although "soothed" is something the patient is supposed to feel, while "untiring" is something the nurse is, and, more importantly, looks. But when *soothing,* as a word, is not alone; when it is jointed, on its side, by two others, then the balance goes out of whack, and the nature of our *and* begins to alter.

patient, submissive, soothing ˍ *untiring*

The *and* we now confront means "finally." It may even mean "and in particular" or "above all." Death, Donne tells us, is a *slave to fate, chance, kings, and* (finally) *desperate men.* This *and,* then, moves from one meaning to another like a pointer on that imaginary scale it has suggested. It begins by intimating equality and balance, but both its position in the series (last), and its separation from the rest (*and* acts as a barrier) increase its importance, as if it were significant enough by itself to weigh as much as the other three. Principally, however, this second *and* indicates the approaching conclusion of a list the way certain symphonic gestures ready us for the culmination of the music. *I love your lips, nose, eyes, hair, chin, and hollow cheeks, your big bank account and bust, my dear.* Balances are delicate, and easily tipped. The social status of a word, its force, its length, its history of use: anything can do it. *The bandit shot my son, stabbed me in the arm, and called me names. What bitter things both life and aspirin are! I've been boating on the Po and Mississippi. You say that your marriage suffers from coital insufficiency and rotten grub? Yeah, my wife kisses her customers and brings their bad breath to bed.*

Between the words *patient* and *submissive,* in the Stein sentence, only a comma intervenes, but that comma stands for an *and* whose presence is purely conceptual. It is *and* become ghostly and bodiless. It is the fatuous gleam in father's eye. Indeed, one could easily write another essay on the germinal, the spermatic character of this seedy, wormlike bit of punctuation. The comma resembles the law, and can command our conscience without a policeman. The absence of the officer is essential to its effect, however, for *she was patient and submissive and soothing and untiring* is another sentence entirely, and not a very forceful one.

To the logician, who is at least patient and untiring, if not soothing and submissive, a connective like *and* or its sometime substitute, the comma, asserts the joint dependency of every element in the pursuit of truth. The logician is outspoken and prefers everything laid out on the bed like clothes for a trip. She (Melanctha) was patient; and she (Melanctha) was submissive; and she (Melanctha) was soothing; and she (Melanctha) was untiring, too—at once and altogether. One can hear what a wearisome way to go at things this is; and for some of the same reason we like our workaday words short and preferably snappy, we fold our ideas over whenever we can—wad them up—and indicate the folds with commas. The logician's assertion of mutual dependency of parts where truth is concerned is paradoxical, and tells us a good deal about *and,* because *and,* whenever it interposes its body, separates each quality from the others and insists that we examine them one at a time, as if they might display themselves on different days or places (as if we were saying that Melanctha was patient on Tuesday, when she wore her bright blue dress, and untiring on Wednesday in her red riding habit, and submissive on Sunday, when she put on her smart pink smock); as if being patient and untiring were conditions that never interpenetrate or affect one another.

The logician's *and* is indifferent to grouping and order. It is all the same to it whether *Bill had a boil on his nose and water in the pot,* or *water in the pot and a boil on his nose,* or whether *Bill has a boil on his nose, water in the pot, and a plant on the sill,* or *a boil on his nose and water in the pot, a plant on the sill with its window on the world.* To our made-up logician, if Melanctha was soothing, then she was soothing, and while we know that she was soothing, we also know she failed to soothe, for Rose Johnson behaved like a simple beast. She was, in good biblical fashion, an abomination. Soothing that is not soothing is not exactly the same as soothing that succeeds and soothes. It is much more likely, in fact, to be infuriating. Who, after all, enjoys being placated: there . . . there. . . .

But the logician is still handy, and reminds us that his *and* (logic being merely a clarification and extension of the male mind even when it is performed by women), lurks unseen by most folks in both *but* and *although*, although *and* is not all of either. *Bill has a boil on his nose, but a window on the world*—a sentence suggesting that Bill, despite his pain, still has a pleasant perspective on things. For that matter, *Bill has water in the pot, although his plant is on the sill.*

In short, in addition to its full appearance as a word, *and* can make itself felt simply as a sound, as in the expression, "canned ham," or it can constitute the underlying meaning of another connective like *but,* or it can exert itself invisibly, as a recurrent idea, a rule of organization. Counting the commas that are stand-ins for it, there are eleven *ands* in Gertrude Stein's sentence.

[*And* #3] *while the sullen, childish, cowardly, black Rosie grumbled and fussed. . . .* Our second *and* drew a list to a close. Certainly *and,* here, suggests that *grumbled* and *fussed* are in balance, but *fussed* will soon be paired with *howled,* and momentarily find itself in a tray belonging to two different scales. As we pass along the list, accumulating the *ands* of *grumbled and fussed and howled and made herself an abomination,* we must constantly shift our weight, first grouping *grumbled* with *fussed,* then *fussed* with *howled,* and finally, with four characteristics at last in place, comparing the first pair of bad behaviors with the second set.

grumbled ₊ fussed   howled ₊ made herself to be an abomination

The specific thing that *fussed* does is add itself to *grumbled,* and the idea of addition, like those of balance, equality, difference, and coordination, is basic to our word, which is often a + sign. *Rosie grumbled, and* (in addition) *fussed.* Additions, of course, can be of many kinds. Sometimes they merely lengthen a list: *Darling: remember to buy Kleenex and coffee and new strings for your mop.* Sometimes, however, they alter its character, change its director, either mildly, as *I love your lips, nose, eyes, hair, chin, and fallen bosom* does, or more radically, as *Duckie, don't forget catsup, kohlrabi, and some conniption, a large can, you know, the kind in sugar syrup* manages, becoming metaphysical. *He lay down and died* does not merely paste death alongside lying down like another stamp in the collection, because, whatever the direction of the other world, death never adds up, although some sentences, such as *he lay down, died, and he rose up again, fresh as a fig and full of spirit,* just might make that suggestion.

I shall return to the concept of the list, to which our *and* will lead us, later.

Every addition implies that somewhere there's a sum. You can't add one number to another—8 to 4, for instance—if the 8 has disappeared by the time the 4 has come round to be counted. However, ordinary actions are like that. I must stop hopping if I'm to skip, and halt all skipping if I'm to jump. My present footstep cannot find the others I have made; even their sound on the sidewalk is gone. So *fussed* adds itself to *grumbled* only in the mind of some observer for whom the sum is one of aggravation. To Melanctha, Rose Johnson grumbled, and (in addition) fussed, and (to top it off) howled. Since Rose did not fuss because she had grumbled, her actions, as external events, merely follow one another in time and replace one another in space, the way Hume indicates our impressions do; and this notion of a simple "next!" is another that is fundamental to the meaning of *and.*

Certain things cannot be added to others because they are already there by implication. To lamb stew you cannot *add* lamb. One adds salt and pepper perhaps. Nor is there any sense in saying that *In addition to being triangular, their love affair had three sides.* Thus, because it is a defining list, in *sullen, childish, cowardly, black Rosie,* the commas do not replace a plus. However, sometimes, to love, one might properly add affection.

Generally, *and* designates only external and unnecessary relations; it deals with incidentals, separables, shoes that slip on and off; but not when it means something like "equally true." *A triangle has three sides and* (it is equally true that) *the sum of its interior angles is 180°.*

[*And* #4] *Rosie grumbled and fussed and howled.* . . . This is the *and* of increasing emphasis. *Rosie grumbled and* (in addition) *fussed and* (what's more) *howled.* It has not lost its coordinate qualities (indeed it is now operating as a pivot between two pairs), and it remains an additive *and* too, but it is now in a place of weight as well. This usually requires that it occupy the last place in any series of conjunctions, and that the items of the set (in this case, names of actions) show a corresponding rise, swell, or increase in scope and importance. You might get away with *Rosie fussed and grumbled and howled,* because it is difficult to regard fussing as any more serious or annoying than grumbling, but you would never get away with *Rosie howled and grumbled and fussed,* unless, of course, you had a special use for that kind of bathos.

The famous lament for Lancelot puts *and* in a brilliant anaphoric series:

Sir Launcelot . . . thou wert never matched of earthly knight's hand; and thou wert the courteoust knight that ever bare shield; and thou wert the truest friend to thy lover that ever bestrad horse; and thou wert the truest lover of sinful man that ever loved woman; and thou wert the kindest man that ever struck with sword; and thou wert the goodliest person that ever came among press of knights; and thou wert the meekest man and the gentlest that ever ate in hall among ladies; and thou were the sternest knight to thy mortal foe that ever put spear in the rest.

Omit the *and* in *knight's hand* and the eight other *ands* that follow it, and you will lose, among other things, the sense of contrast between qualities that the conjunction heightens, the sense, throughout, of characteristics coexisting *despite* one another: *fire and ice.*

[*And* #5] *and made herself to be an abomination. . . .* Our fifth *and,* since it appears in series with *ands* #3 and #4, begins by signaling that it is another addition with emphasis. Indeed, it starts to withdraw some of #4's culminating force, for it is seen, now, not quite to culminate. However, the expression that follows the fifth *and* is not a single verb, which its normal coordinating function would lead us to expect anyway, but an entire clause. Furthermore, while *howling, fussing,* and *grumbling* are intransitive verbs, *making* is not. I said a moment ago that addition implies a sum, and here it is: the summarizing, totalizing *and. Rosie grumbled and fussed and howled and* (altogether) *made herself to be an abomination. . . .*

[*And* #6] *and like a simple beast.* Our final explicit *and* does not occur in a balancing position. Although it is in series, that series, as we have moved through it, has been undergoing transformations. *Fussed* is added to *grumbled,* then *howled* is emphatically attached, and these add up to *abomination.* Now this sum is interpreted and explained by resorting to the *and* of equivalence, to the *and* of "that is to say." *She made herself to be an abomination and* (that is to say) *like a simple beast.*

So far, we have considered these *ands* as if they existed in relative isolation, in terms of their local impact upon one another, and not in terms of the total effect of their use. But six *ands* have surfaced in this sentence. Each one comes between its companions like a referee. Within more prepositional phrases, for instance, the sense of things follows the reading eye from left to right as seems proper. *Look—at the little dog— in its cute pink angora sweater.* Because, in such formations, the so-called minor and undominate connectors come first, meaning moves toward *dog,* then *sweater* like a drain, although with all those adjectives piled up in the second phrase, the drain begins to clog. But our *ands* part their elements while retaining them. They divvy, weigh, equalize, and order. They spread their objects out like dishes on a table. *And look at the little, and at the little dog, and at its cute and pink and fuzzy angora sweater.* Innocence is thick as custard here, because *and* is an enemy of "subordination." It appears (although this, as we saw, is illusory) . . . it appears to be unspecific and sloppy, to replace definitely understood connections with vaguely indistinct ones; hence it is frequently found in unstudied and childlike speech, or in regressive and harried circum-stances. *I saw a snake and it was long and black and slithery and fork-tongued and pepper-eyed and slimy and evil and a cliché in the grass.* Although such a sentence generates plenty of forward motion, most of it is due to the breathlessness implied by the repeated use of the conjunc-tion, and not by its separative and spacializing function.

   In the following example, Ernest Hemingway, Gertrude Stein's under-study, is working for a kind of fuddled bewilderment and frightened ener-gy by a deliberate misuse of the word. The narrator in the story, "After the Storm," has just knifed a man in a bar.

Well, I went out of there and there were plenty of them with him and some came out after me and I made a turn and was down by the docks and I met a fellow and he said somebody killed a man up the street. I said "Who killed him?" and he said "I don't know who killed him but he's dead all right," and it was dark and there was water standing in the street and no lights and windows broke and boats all up in the town and trees blown down and everything all blown and I got a skiff and went out and found my boat where I had her inside of Mango Key and she was all right only she was full of water. So I bailed her out and pumped her out and there was a moon but plenty of clouds and still plenty rough and I took it down along; and when it was daylight I was off Eastern Harbor.

These *ands* do not establish parallels or connections; they suggest chasms. Between one act and another—between turning a corner and meeting a man—there is nothing. These *ands* condense or skip. They insist upon the suddenness of everything, the disappearance of time, the collision of distant spaces. Of course, these are the *ands* of nervousness, too, of worry and sleeplessness, of sheep leaping fences one after another. They cause events to ricochet.[4]

Ands

are almost essential for excess. They are perfect if you want to make big piles or imply an endless addition. One *and* may make a tidy pair, closing a couple like a snap: *War and Peace, ham and eggs, Pride and Prejudice*. Add another and then another, however, and the third *and* will begin to alter the earlier ones the same miraculous way the squashed and flattened condition named by *mashed* is lent the fully contrasting sense of *heaped* simply by putting it nearby the word *potato*. No one is any better at this energetic mounding than the Dickens of *Dombey*. Here is part of a long passage describing the ruination of a neighborhood by some newlaid railroad tracks. It implies he is not telling us the half of it:

There were frowzy fields, and cow-houses, and dunghills and dustheaps, and ditches, and gardens, and summerhouses, and carpet-beating grounds, at the very door of the railway. Little tumuli of oyster shells in the oyster season, and of lobster shells in the lobster season, and of broken crockery and faded cabbage leaves in all seasons, encroached upon its high places. Posts, and rails, and old cautions to trespassers, and backs of mean houses, and patches of wretched vegetation, stared it out of countenance.

There is the *and* that enumerates things and conditions, as here, and helps to heap them up; and there is the *and* that multiplies names and descriptions, creating a verbal heap instead, as we frequently find in Rabelais, master of all middens, and of every excess the celebrant, and extoller, and rhapsodist.

If we momentarily return, now, to the first *and* of Gertrude Stein's set of six, we can see that it attaches the entire remainder of our sentence to the initial *She tended Rose*. . . . This *and* is both adverbial, as we saw, informing us how well and kindly Melanctha took care of Rose, but it is adversarial in additional, setting Melanctha's conduct sharply over against Rose's (who becomes "Rosie" when we learn of her low-class

4. Frederick Busch discusses a part of this passage and makes some similar points in "Icebergs, Islands, Ships beneath the Sea," in *Insights I: Working Papers in Contemporary Criticism, a John Hawkes Symposium* (New York: New Directions, 1977), pp. 51–52.

ways). So our specimen is made of an opening clause (*She tended Rose. . . .*) and a closing phrase (*. . . like a simple beast*) that precisely balances it, while between these two segments three four-term series are sung, one that belongs to Melanctha, and two that belong to Rose and describe first her character and then her behavior. At this point we encounter an *and* (also operative in the Dickens sample) that has its home within the rhetorical structure itself, for it is as if the sentence's shape said that Melanctha was patient and Rose was sullen; Melanctha was submissive and Rose was childish, and so on, employing the *and* of simultaneity, of *while. Gricks may rise and Troysers fall,* Joyce writes, using the same connective. Sullen Rosie grumbled, the rhetorical form says; childish Rosie fussed; cowardly black Rosie howled and made herself to be an abomination and like a simple beast—a structure that invokes the *and* of consequence and cause. *I bought some stock in IBM and the bottom of the market parted like a wet sock.*

Dickens, by repeating *oyster shells in the oyster season and lobster shells in the lobster season,* not only collects these two kinds of shells in the same place, his *and* identifies the two rhetorical formulas in which these four little tumuli of shells and crockery and cabbage leaves are given to us. So there are *ands* that vary in their meanings, and *ands* that differ in terms of the kinds of objects they connect: things, inscriptions, concepts, or syntactical shapes and rhetorical patterns.

In the single sentence I took from Gertrude Stein, we have now found six overt *ands*, each with a different dominate meaning; five covert *ands*, which hid themselves unsuccessfully under commas; and two *ands* which were implied by the form. Nor does this list (itself an *and* producing format) even remotely exhaust the various senses, sometimes several at the same time, that these thirteen *ands* possess, nor did my account even minimally describe the interaction between different meanings that any one written or spoken token might represent, or do more than suggest something of the dynamics of switching and sliding senses, as readings were anticipated, accepted, revised, rejected, retained. And we have only to glance again at the passage from Hemingway to find meanings for the word we haven't yet examined. You may recall the peculiar formation: *Well, I went out of there and there were plenty of them with him. . . .* This is the *and* of consequence, in this case inverted so that it becomes an *and* of tardy explanation, the *and* of belated *because.*

The narrator got out of there *because* the man he knifed had plenty of friends with him.

And

sometimes means "in company" or "together with," as *the passengers and all their luggage were hurled from the plane*. And *Dombey and Son*.

And

sometimes means "we may call these things by the same name, but the differences among them are often important and profound," as *there are doctors and doctors*. This use may be regarded as a particularly pronounced example of the differentiating, or "over against" *and*.

And

sometimes means "remember all the incidents, events, ideas, that came before, or just before, this," as in the famous opening of Pound's *Cantos*.

> *And then went down to the ship,*
> *Set keel to breakers, forth on the godly sea, and*
> *We set up mast and sail on that swart ship,*
> *Bore sheep aboard her, and our bodies also*
> *Heavy with weeping, and winds from sternward*
> *Bore us out onward with bellying canvas,*
> *Circe's this craft, the trim-coiffed goddess.*

And

is sometimes used in the spirit of "you might not believe it, but . . ." and as if in answer to an unspoken question. *And yes, we did set up mast and sail on that swart ship*. Or, *at the half we had a ten point lead, and we still lost by two touchdowns*. Or, *and we ate human flesh!*

Often dangled or uncoupled *and* expresses surprise or indignation. It is an emphatic form of the remember-what-came-before *and*. *And you talk to me this way, after all I've done for you?* Here the *and* of consequence has suffered a familiar disappointment. Or, *so Peking; and do you now go to Moscow?*

There are several rather antique *ands*: the *and* of fourscore and seven, the *and* of *I'll love you forever and ever*, or *we'll get together by and by.* More ancient is the *and* that sometimes substitutes for the number of times, as *they boarded the ark two and two,* or *the room was only ten and ten,* now rarely resorted to, and replaced by *by.*

There is the *and* that turns the initial member of a coordinate pair into an adverb. In *the fire kept them nice and warm,* "nicely warm" is meant. But "nicely warm" is not a synonym because the *and* allows the fire to keep them nice, as if at any moment they might dry out and get tough, or evil and mean. There is also the *and* that replaces the infinitive: *why don't you come up and see me some time?* Again, this is not simply a mindless replacement for the apparently more precise: *why don't you come up to see me,* because *and* equalizes *coming* and *seeing* and removes the rather insistent statement of purpose—especially important here, where seeing is probably only the first—shoeless—step.

Around some expressions there hover an astonishing number of ghostly forms, whiffs, sibilant suggestions, vague intimations, and these, as well as the more overt relationships that the reader is expected to grasp as a matter of course, help give them a feeling of classic correctness. Mae West's famous invitation, *why don't you come up and see me some time,* with its careful softening of a command into a question, alters the cliché—*you folks come back and see me soon, you hear?*— basically by only one word—*up*—and that change suggests "bedroom" to my bad ear, while *come up* suggests "erection." *Come* suggests "climax," *see me* sounds like "seize me," and "seed me," and so on, so that the *and* it contains hums like a tuning fork between all these fainter and further thoughts and their terms. Mae West's seductive delivery, of course, lets us know how we are to hear her invitation, but *up* is the verbal pointer that prepares us to flush these remaining meanings within range of our gun.

Logical and grammatical form—the fact that *and* is a connective and not an article, an adjective, or a noun—limit somewhat the meanings that our word may assume, but only somewhat, and there is little in these formal dispositions that can tell us in advance of experience what *and* means. We can't even know whether we are going to be dealing with a preposition, a conjunction, or a strange kind of adverb; yet the ordinary reader is able to distinguish one use of *and* from another with an ease that never causes us any astonishment: the syntax takes shape simultaneously with the meanings it shapes.

For we know what it is to take care of someone. We know what it is to be patient. We have seen patient caring, and the irritable, impatient kind (we can even imagine impatient patience, as if one were in a hurry to get this period of placid absorbancy and affable putting-up-with over with), so that when the words call our experiences together in a sentence, the ensuing arrangement, and completed meaning, is the result of our memories of life and our understanding of language. Patience has a history as a human condition which I've encountered before and occasionally enjoyed; and the word *patience* has a career as a concept and a mark that I myself have seen and heard and written down and uttered. It is the same, to a degree, with all words. That is, I remember the meanings; I remember my encounters with their referents; and I remember the company of other words that the ones in question have commonly kept. However, when I remember these things, I do not remember serially one fact or feeling, one usage, at a time, as if I were thumbing through an index or flipping through a file. These memories have been compacted and their effects summed, although I may recollect my mother's patience during one trying time with particular distinctness, or recall the famous "now patience" passage in *Finnegans Wake* more readily than others. My mind remembers the way trained muscles do, so when I speak and read as well as I walk and bike, then we can say that I have incorporated my language; it has become another nature, an organlike facility; and *that* language, at least, will have been invested with meaning, not merely assigned it. I may have just learned that *ne plus ultra* signifies an ultimate or utmost point; nevertheless, the phrase will still stand aside from its referent like politeness at a doorway—but when, for me, idea and object fuse with their sign, then the sign is valuable like the coin it resembles; it is alive, a unity of mind and body that can be taught to sing, to dance.

The sentence describing my cat as she rests on her little woven mat or the one telling of the ten dollars I've put on some poor nag's nose: each will calmly present their respective facts on the same sort of plate: X on Y; just as *Samson and Delilah, gin and tonic, spit 'n polish, hem and haw,* will wear identical black ties as if they were going to the same dance. And if we did not understand the meaning of the word that fills these forms, we might then imagine my money balanced precariously on the nose of a galloping pony, or consider *hem and haw* to headline a comedy team, a couple of hillbillies, or a famous pair of lovers like *sweet and low.* However, my experience of things by itself will not suffice to explain my understanding of Gertrude Stein's sentence, or, for that matter, any other. I must know where *and* has been; I must be familiar with the way *and* works; and just as I understand how patience as a quality of behavior is modified by its surroundings, while, in turn, modifying them, so I have to be similarly ready to pick up every nuance of the interaction between terms. Sometimes one of these dimensions of a word's nature—in terms of its history or my memory—will be much shorter than another. For instance, in the movies, I may have seen native beaters driving game toward the hidden white hunters (I see trembling honeys, fair-haired heroes, sullen sahibs), but I may not know the word for this action, which is *battue*. Or I may have a reasonable notion of what *bar mitzvah* means without ever having attended a mitzvah of any kind. And there are many ideas (along with the words that represent them, such as *bathometry*) which refer to practices I've never attempted, or to instruments I've never used that I nevertheless grasp well enough. Still, wherever my life is lacking in such encounters, or a word or thing is shy, or secretive, or excessively selective, or reprehensible or ugly, then that word will lag behind or limp along among the regiments of others. The suggestion that we use the language of ordinary men is a good one, normally, not simply because we shall reach the ear and understanding of ordinary men that way (which remains unlikely), but because such words are rich with history, both in our life and in theirs, and shine throughout with smoothness like stones that have, for vast ages, been tossed back and forth in the surf of some ancient shore, becoming eloquent, as pebbles made the mouth of Demosthenes hiss and seeth and roar. *And* is such a polished orb. Think of the places it has been, the shoulders it has rubbed, the connections it has had, the meanings it has absorbed, the almost limitless future that yet awaits!

And

if we were suddenly to speak of the *andness* of things, we would be rather readily understood to refer to that aspect of life that consists of just one damned *and* after another. *And* is a desperate part of speech precisely because it separates and joins at the same time. It equalizes. Neither ham nor eggs are more or less. In *donkey and dragons* the donkey brings the dragon down, while *sweet cream and a kiss* manages an elevation.

And

so what? The inner order of the *and* is the list, to which we must now turn—that field where all its objects at least implicitly rest. Here is a brief list of lists: the list that is made up of reminders, shorthand commands—get *X*, do *Y*, check *Z*—such as the grocery or shopping list, the list of things to get done before leaving for Europe, before ignition and lift off, before embarking upon a prolonged affair; and there are want lists, Christmas lists, and so on, much the same; then there is the inventory, and the catalog, the bests and the worsts, restaurants deserving two stars and three forks, statistical tables and other compilations, directories, almanacks, hit lists, dictionaries, deportation orders, delightfully sheer enumerations. Some lists are as disorderly as laundry—that is, only somewhat—or as chaotic as one made for marketing, ordered only as items pop into the mind, or as supplies run out, and having no real first, middle, most, or honest end. Sometimes particular items will be underscored or starred. Certain *ands* (the *and* for emphasis, for instance) often operate like an asterisk. Other arrangements are neutral and simply for convenience, as book lists are often alphabetical. The factors of 8 could be listed in any order without real prejudice, although I prefer $1 + 2 + 4 + 8$ to other, more slipshoddy, renditions. Occasionally a bookdealer will shelve his books according to author only, instead of by title or subject matter, and then the catlog's alphabetical simplicity and the structure of the corresponding state of affairs in his shop will be the same.

Among the organizing principles of lists, then, are (1) things simply come upon, either the way they are remembered, as a guest list may be composed, or as found, for instance, when the police inventory your pockets before putting you away; (2) items listed in accordance with some external principle, often so that things can be easily located—for instance, numerically, alphabetically, astrologically, regimentally, hermeneutically; and (3) as dictated by the order of things themselves, like a book's table of contents, or vice versa, as when the library's catalog shelves the books and commands their connections. We must suppose that God's list of things to do (on the first day—light, on the second day—land, on the third day—life, and so on) possessed a hidden internal principal, and there may be other self-generating lists of this kind.

William Gass

Lists are juxtapositions, and often employ some of the techniques of collage. The collage, of course, brings strangers together, uses its *ands* to suggest an affinity without specifying what it is, and produces thereby a low-level but general nervousness. It is one of the essential elements of a truly contemporary style. Lists—full of *ands* as they are—remove things from their normal place, not as an artist might, by picking up a piece of paper from the street to paste upon a canvas (as the romance maintains), but by substituting for such found objects their names, and then rearranging those. As a consequence, lists are dominated by nouns. Here is a little list of words of the sort that rarely appear on lists: *always* is never there, nor *nevermore,* nor *if* (although there is the expression, *don't give me any ifs, ands, or buts*); less than occasionally, *subjugation, half-heartedly, yeah,* or *Lithuaneousness.* Even some nouns, like *junta,* manage to stay quite away. However, adjectives of a usefully descriptive kind—those quiet, unassuming servants of nouns— frequently appear: yellow cheese, large eggs, fresh milk, bitten nails.

That part of punctuation most associated with lists is therefore the colon, for presumably everything that follows *it* is a list. The several meanings of the word are thought by some to have no familial connections. Nevertheless, the comedians persevere. As we know, the colon is frequently an abbreviation for *namely,* or *for instance.* There are thirteen ways of looking at a blackbird: (namely) on Sunday, in the yellowing woods, with a friend, following a thin fall rain, and so forth.

Lists sometimes suggest or supply alternatives, not necessarily exclusive; for example, ways of getting spots off tea trays, or means of travel that avoid Cleveland. They supply possibilities: the people who could ride on the cowcatcher, the games you could play in a stadium: roller skating the ramps, playing checkers on an empty seat, hide and seek. If I am drawing up a list of physical attitudes or comportments surprisingly suitable for sex, although there is an implicit *and* standing between each (while learning wearily against your partner like the man with the hoe, as though sitting slowly down upon a hassock), it is not expected that you will put all of these to use one after another as though loading groceries in a cart. These *ands* resemble *or* more than they resemble themselves.

Lists have subjects. They are possessive. Lists are lists of. There is the list of foodstuffs needed for the ascent of Everest; there is the ruck one finds in a rucksack, items up for auction, wines and prices; while the little leaflet, the roster sheet, the penciled-in dance card, the back of an old envelope on which a list has been made: each of these symbolizes the tabletop or field or sorting tray, rucksack or room, where we may imagine these items have been assembled. This is sometimes called "the site."

Since a list has a subject to which its items are constantly referred, it suppresses its verb (to buy, to remind, to count, to store), and tends to retard the forward movement of the mind. We remain on the site. While the early *ands* of a series propel us onward, the later ones run breathlessly in place; thus the list (as we have seen) is a fundamental device for creating a sense of overflow, abundance, excess. We find it almost invariably so used in Rabelais, and often in Cervantes. Why name one thing when you can invoke many? Why be merely thirsty, why simply drink, when you can cry out with Grangousier: "I wet, I dampen, I moisten, I humect my gullet, I drink—and all for fear of dying of aridity!" Here, however, our list is not one of alternative actions, but of additional *words*. I could say "moisten my gullet"; or I could say "dampen my gullet"; but, by the cerebral swillings of all the sophists, I shall say both, and more, in order to suggest the generous great gulp of life I am presently swallowing. Who, indeed, could be satisfied to say, of the breasts of their beloved, simply that they are as white and soft as a hillock of junket? *Rhumen, dass ist!*

Rabelais is also full of lists of rapid talk, dialogue that does not advance the subject at all, but rather fills it, as drink does the bladder. Topers sail away in a wind of words, they do not huff and puff along highways, swim Hellesponts. Then there are the slanging matches, bouts of name-calling and bad mouthing: you, sir, are a snerd; and you, sir, are a gurp, and you, snerd, are a suckalini, and you, gurp, are a goofballoof! One remembers, with fondness, the two whores and their name-calling contest in *The Sot Weed Factor*.

Lists, then, are for those who savor, who revel and wallow, who embrace not only the whole of things but all of its accounts, histories, descriptions, justifications. They are for those who like, in every circumstance, to Thomas Wolfe things down, to whoop it, Whitmanly, up. *Ands* run from Wolfe as if he were a faucet for them.

And before and after that, and in between, and in and out, and during it and later on, and now and then, and here and there, and at home and abroad, and on the

William Gass

seven seas, and across the length and breadth of the five continents, and yesterday and tomorrow and forever—could it be said of her that she had been promiscuous?

Even the jeremiad is a list, and full of joy. Damnations are delightful. Lists are finally for those who love language, the vowel-swollen cheek, the lilting, dancing tongue, because lists are fields full of words, and roving bands of *and*. Life itself can only be compiled and thereby captured on a list, if it can be laid out anywhere at all, especially if you are a nominalist. Perhaps impressions can be caught like butterflies and pinned. Here's a pungent-blue-loud-sour-scratchy collection, and then another, yellow-sweet this time (but aren't they all complex?), and yet another, of course, a pale-tart-pink-and-screaming-hotspot, wow! I shall have to stretch the parchment with my teeth to take these endless droplets down.

List-making is a form of collecting, of course, conservative in that sense, and dictionaries are the noblest lists of all; but lists are ubiquitous in literature. It is not merely Walt Whitman who is made of them. They are as frequent a rhetorical element as *and* is a grammatical one. We could scarcely write much without either. When do we have a list, however, and when not? There is no limit, presumably, to the length of lists so long as they have one, for the idea of a list implies the possibility of a complete enumeration. I may not have completed my list of all the cars with Delaware license plates that have stopped at my gas station, but an end is in sight, for my cancer is incurable and the station will soon close. I cannot make a list of all the odd numbers, only the ones, say, I like. There are an infinite number of numbers that no one will ever name. My mentioning five trillion and seven, now, will not make a dent in them. A daunting thought. It is sometimes naively supposed that those unnamed numbers will either be unimaginably huge (galaxies of googolplexes) or terrifyingly tiny (pi, pied), but there are almost certainly neglected numbers of no particular distinction hidden in the shadows of others, which chance has simply skipped. Another daunting thought. So lists must be *of a length*. When Rabelais tells us what little Gargantua did between the ages of 3 and 5, the entire chapter becomes an enumeration of the characteristics and qualities, the deeds, of this Herculean tyke.

> Fat? another ounce of wind and he would have exploded.
> Appreciative? He would piss, full-bladdered, at the sun.
> Cautious? He used to hide under water for fear of the rain.

120

But when we write nothing but "Kleenex" on the flap of our envelope, we haven't a list yet, though we may have begun to make one; it awaits the *and*. *Kleenex and cauliflower* is only a pair, and pairs are opposed to lists, and close upon themselves like clapping hands (though I wonder what sound this pair would make when they came together), while *Kleenex, cauliflower, and catnip* is simply a skimpy plurality. Alliteration actually makes the three items seem more numerous than they are, so I think that with four such we can say our list has truly begun. When I wrote down *catnip*, I did not add it to a list, for there wasn't a list yet; but now that we have one, variously things can be said to be *on* or *off* it, or eligible for inclusion or not. The phrase, *fate, chance, kings, and desperate men* forms a list. Notice, however, that until there was a list, *fate*, like *catnip* before, was not on it; but that, once the list was made, *fate*, we see, was always on. One other oddity: there may be lists that exist mainly in an ideal realm, and that are rarely realized. Maybe I've made a list of what I need to get at the grocer's: Kleenex, chicken wings, Twinkies, fruit; when actually what I really need are lemons, vitamins, and thighs. I've forgotten Chuckie's cat food, too, so my list isn't even a list of what *I* want. Actually, I really need Rye Crisp and bottled water. When I initially collect the qualities that create a character, don't I often discard some and add others, as if, all along, I am searching for the *right* list? *Fate, chance, kings, and desperate men* is certainly a correct one. But we had better back away from this *mysterium tremens.*

There are some lists one wants rather desperately to be on: the Honor Roll, for instance; but some should be shunned, like the Lord High Executioner's little list of people who surely won't be missed, or that other roll call way up yonder for which one does not wish to be eligible just yet.

Although the list by itself is a small democracy, and usually lacks hierarchies (the 1003 women on Don Giovanni's are, presumably, all loved equally by the list, if not by the Don), when the list occurs in a literary work, these conditions change, and the order of items becomes especially important. Ah hah! Holmes exclaims, our suspect has put down *catnip* before *Kleenex*. Of course, like Holmes's cases, works of literature suffer from an excess of the essential. The normal democracy of lists is connected with the coordinating and balancing functions of *and*, as well as its additive and merely enumerative character: *How do I love thee, let me count the ways* . . . yet even the *ands* of emphasis, or of *finally*, or *in sum*, introduce certain small subordinations, the importance

William Gass

of every *and,* and the elements it connects, even its pecking orders, remains substantially the same.

I've pointed out that listing things, or inserting an *and* between them, can only be done by replacing the things with their names, and thereby transforming their relations. If you are moving, and have made a list of your belongings so that the insurance company can repay you when the wagons are lost crossing the mountains, the spacial relation between these objects (between hairbrush and table, table and footstool, footstool and rug) will be replaced (as it just was) with a simple serial relation between indifferent nouns that find their rest, now, only on a yellow sheet. The rug, on which I lay as a baby to have my naked picture taken, will be listed in the same way as yours—one woolly rug—though it was there you lost your virginity, and he lay one tan hand beneath the frillies of your tennis dress, and—. Nothing but a list can restore such moments to us. A list can calmly take apart a chair, and reduce its simultaneous assemblage to a song: back, leg, cushion, square feet, embroidery, grease spot, saggy spring, slight scratch, small tear, lost tack. If I cut up an action for inclusion on a list, I shall have to divide it the way the flight of Zeno's arrow was divided, and a continuum will become an enumeration. *He ran rapidly forward, leaped, and comfortably cleared the hurdle* makes three acts out of what was once one, and these segments can be moved about like beans. *Landing awkwardly on his left leg, he knew his run had been rapid enough for his leap at least to clear the hurdle.* What has been divided, here, is no longer an action, but a memory. Indeed, I can cut up the action in a lot of ways, slicing *He ran rapidly forward* into a stride with the right foot, a stride with the left, and so on, even becoming microscopic: *shove off right, lift, swing, extend, plant, pull,* etc., and in this way never reaching, any more than Achilles does, the hurdle. The camera is such a list-maker, because a film is essentially a series of stills, temporally arranged and uniformly flashed so as to restore continuity at the price of illusion.

Borges, who has made some of our more memorable lists, refers at one point to a "certain Chinese encyclopedia" in which it is written that

animals are divided into (a) belonging to the Emperor, (b) embalmed, (c) tame, (d) sucking pigs, (e) sirens, (f) fabulous, (g) stray dogs, (h) included in the present classification, (i) frenzied, (j) innumerable, (k) drawn with a very fine camelhair brush, (l) *et cetera,* (m) having just broken the water pitcher, (n) that from a long way off look like flies;

122

and Michel Foucault, who claims this passage and the laughter it pro-
voked, were the source of his book, *The Order of Things,* says we cannot
imagine the kind of place where these creatures could be brought together and sorted out. The site is impossible to conceive. He says that
the encyclopedia, "and the taxonomy it proposes, lead to a kind of
thought without space, to words and categories that lack all life and
place, but are rooted in a ceremonial space, overburdened with complex figures, with tangled paths, strange places, secret passages, and
unexpected communications." We read the congregation of these rid-
dling words, but is there anywhere a sack that will sometime fill with such
groceries?

And

always raises this issue as if it were a flag for waving. *Bread* and *honey*
meet at the breakfast table as easily as husband and wife; they are both
with us in our world, and cause scarcely a blink; but what keeps *carrot*
and *cruelty* together beside *c*? Every list has a length, a purpose, an
order, its own entrance requirements, its own principles of exclusion, its
site. Foucault has not felt the point of the Chinese encyclopedia's list, so
he cannot conceive of its site, but Borges does not mean merely to con-
found and delight us with this crazy classification; for, at another level, it
represents a well-chosen series of logical mistakes. It is a collection of
examples, and is not to be taken any more literally than, let's say, remarks about the cross and the crown should be thought to be simply
about crowns and crosses.

The Chinese world, we think, is upside down? Very well. So is this list.
The classes it names aren't workably exclusive, but badly overlap: birds
belonging to the emperor might be tamed or embalmed, and if so, they
are certainly "included in the present classification." Live dogs, stuffed
deer, mythological monsters, are grouped so aggressively they chal-
lenge the presumably overriding importance of other distinctions—that
between the real and the imaginary, for instance, or the alive and the
dead. Still, as widely as its net is thrown, there are too many holes in it;
most wild animals will easily elude its cast, and it omits mention of those
animals whose names have never been used to characterize football
teams. The groups are too specific in some cases, too general in others.
It offers us categories that cannot be applied, others that are vague,
wholly subjective, or disastrously self-referential. In short, each example

attacks some part of the logical structure of the list, and this is what, wonderlandlike, it is a list of. It may seem to suggest that there are more things in heaven and earth than are dreamt of in our eaxonomies, but Borges provides us with a possible reality behind that appearance. The site of this list is in an introductory text in logic—somewhere in the chapter on classification.

One can sense what *and* is up to by examining writers and passages that use it sparely, or exclude it altogether, as Beckett characteristically does, especially in later works like *How It Is,* because it is precisely the dissolution and denial of identities he wishes to stress. When, very rarely, the word appears, it either stands between terms only verbally different (*with me someone there with me still and me there still*) or when *and* is used to equalize life and death (*the voice stops for one or the other reason and life along with it above in the light and we along with it that is what becomes of us*).

Can one word make a world? Of course not. God said: *es werde Licht,* not "*Licht*" alone.[5] But when an *and* appears between any two terms, as we have seen, a place where these two "things" belong together has been implied. Furthermore, the homogeneity of chaos, *ohne Form und leer,* has been sundered, for we must think of chaos, *Tiefe,* not as a helterskelter of worn-out and broken or halfheartedly realized things like a junkyard or potter's midden, but as a fluid mishmash of thinglessness in every lack of direction, as if a blender had run amok.

And

is that sunderer; it divides into new accords; it stands between *Himmel und Erde*; it divides light from darkness.

And

again moves between sea and sky and their several waters, so that a new relationship arises between them, one that is external and unencumbering, although intimate as later will be Eve and Adam. Dividing earth from ocean, grass from earth, summer from winter and night from day, is again: *and.*

5. It is my suspicion that God speaks German.

And

those that crawl are otherwise than those that fly because of it. Finally, of course, between Himself and Himself there came a glass, a gleaming image: God and man, then. And among the male and the female, and within man, the soul and life and mind and body, were sorted and set, as though in left and right hands, beside but separate from one another.

then God went away to other delights, *an Reiz und Kraft,* leaving us with our days and nights and other downfalls, our sites and lists and querulous designs and petty plans, our sentiments and insatiables and dreamlands, with the problem of other minds, with the spirit's unhappy household in the body, with essences and accidents and no insurance, with all those bilious and libelous tongues, pissing angels, withheld rewards, broken promises, all those opportunities for good and evil, sex, marriage, world wars, work, and worship—and with *and*: a sword that cleaves things as it cleaves them.

And

then some.

Apple, Max

The Oranging of America. New York: Grossman Publishers, 1976.
Zip: A Novel of the Left and the Right. New York: Viking Press, 1978.
Free Agents. New York: Harper & Row, 1984.

Barthelme, Donald

Come Back, Dr. Caligari. Boston: Little, Brown, & Co., 1964.
Snow White. New York: Atheneum, 1967.
Unspeakable Practices, Unnatural Acts. New York: Farrar, Straus and Giroux, 1968.
City Life. New York: Farrar, Straus & Giroux, 1970.
Sadness. New York: Farrar, Straus & Giroux, 1972.
Guilty Pleasures. New York: Farrar, Straus & Giroux, 1975.
The Dead Father. New York: Farrar, Straus & Giroux, 1975.
Amateurs. New York: Farrar, Straus & Giroux, 1976.
Great Days. New York: Farrar, Straus & Giroux, 1979.
Sixty Stories. New York: E.P. Dutton, Inc., 1981.
Overnight to Many Distant Cities. New York: Putnam, 1983.

Betts, Doris

The Gentle Insurrection. New York: Putnam, 1954.
Tall Houses in Winter. New York: Putnam, 1957.

The Scarlet Thread. New York: Harper & Row, 1964.

The Astronomer and Other Stories. New York: Harper & Row, 1966.

The River to Pickle Beach. New York: Harper & Row, 1972.

Beasts of the Southern Wild and Other Stories. New York: Harper & Row, 1973.

Heading West. New York: Alfred Knopf, Inc., 1981.

▬▬▬

Garrett, George

The Reverend Ghost. New York: Scribner, 1957.

King of the Mountain. New York: Scribner, 1958.

The Sleeping Gypsy and Other Poems. Austin: University of Texas Press, 1958.

The Finished Man. New York: Scribner, 1960.

Which Ones Are the Enemy. New York: Little, Brown & Co., Inc., 1961.

In the Briar Patch. Austin: University of Texas Press, 1961.

Abraham's Knife. North Carolina: University of North Carolina Press, 1961.

Cold Ground Was My Bed Last Night. Columbia: University of Missouri Press, 1964.

Do Lord Remember Me. Garden City, New York: Doubleday & Co., Inc., 1964.

The Girl In The Black Raincoat. New York: Duell, Sloan & Pearce, 1965.

For A Bitter Season. Columbia: University of Missouri Press, 1967.

A Wreath for Garibaldi. London: Rupert Hart-Davies, 1969.

The Death of the Fox. Garden City, New York: Doubleday & Co., Inc., 1971.

The Magic Striptese. New York: Doubleday & Co., Inc., 1973.

Botteghe Oscure Reader. Middletown, Connecticutt: Wesleyan University Press, 1974.

Luck's Shining Child. Winston-Salem: Palaemon Press, 1981.

The Succession. Garden City, New York: Doubleday & Co., Inc., 1983.

The Collected Poems of George Garrett. Fayetteville: University of Arkansas Press, 1984.

James Jones. San Diego: Harcourt Brace Jovanovich, 1984.

An Evening Performance. New York: Doubleday & Co., Inc., 1985.

Gass, William

Omensetter's Luck. New York: New American Library, Inc., 1966.
In the Heart of the Heart of the Country. New York: Harper & Row, 1968.
Fiction and the Figures of Life. Boston: Nonpareil Books, 1971.
Willie Master's Lonesome Wife. Evanston, Ill.: Northwestern University Press, 1968. New York: Knopf, 1971.
On Being Blue. Boston: Godine, 1976.
The World Within the Word. New York: Knopf, 1978.
Habitations of the Word. New York: Simon & Schuster, 1985.

Irving, John

Setting Free the Bears. New York: Random House, 1968.
The Water-Method Man. New York: Random House, 1972.
The 158-Pound Marriage. New York: Random House, 1974.
The World According to Garp. New York: E. P. Dutton, 1978.
3 By Irving. New York: Random House, 1980.
The Hotel New Hampshire. New York: E. P. Dutton, 1981.
The Cider House Rules. New York: William Morrow & Co., 1985.

Morris, Wright

NOVELS

My Uncle Dudley. Lincoln: University of Nebraska Press, 1942.
The Man Who Was There. Lincoln: University of Nebraska Press, 1945.
The World in the Attic. New York: Charles Scribner's Sons, 1949.
Man and Boy. Lincoln: University of Nebraska Press, 1951.
The Works of Love. Lincoln: University of Nebraska Press, 1951.
The Deep Sleep. New York: Scribner, 1953.
The Huge Season. New York: Viking Press, 1954.
The Field of Vision. New York: Harcourt Brace Jovanovich, 1956.
Love Among the Cannibals. New York: Harcourt Brace Jovanovich, 1957.

What a Way to Go. New York: Atheneum, 1962.
Cause for Wonder. New York: Atheneum, 1963.
One Day. Lincoln: University of Nebraska Press, 1965.
In Orbit. Lincoln: University of Nebraska Press, 1969.
Fire Sermon. Lincoln: University of Nebraska Press, 1971.
War Games. Lincoln: University of Nebraska Press, 1972.
A Life. Lincoln: University of Nebraska Press, 1973.
Ceremony in Lone Tree. Lincoln: University of Nebraska Press, 1973.
The Fork River Space Project. New York: Harper and Row, 1977.
Plains Song. New York: Harper and Row, 1980.

PHOTO-TEXTS

The Inhabitants. New York, Charles Scribner's Sons, 1946.
The Home Place. Lincoln: University of Nebraska Press, 1948.
God's Country and My People. New York: Harper and Row, 1968.
Love Affair: A Venetian Journal. n.p., n.d.
Photographs and Words. Carmel, California: Friends of Photography, 1982.

ESSAY COLLECTIONS

The Territory Ahead. New York: Atheneum, 1958.
A Bill of Rites, A Bill of Wrongs, A Bill of Goods. New York: New American Library, 1968.
About Fiction.
Earthly Delights, Unearthly Adornments. New York: Harper & Row, 1978.

SHORT STORY COLLECTION

Real Losses, Imaginary Gains. New York: Harper & Row, 1976.

MEMOIRS

Will's Boy. New York: Harper & Row, 1981.
Solo. New York: Harper & Row, 1983.
A Cloak of Light. New York: Harper & Row, 1985.

——————

Smith, Lee

The Last Day the Dogbushes Bloomed. New York: Harper & Row, 1968.
Something in the Wind. New York: Harper & Row, 1971.

Fancy Strut. New York: Harper & Row, 1973.
Black Mountain Breakdown. New York: Ballentine Books, 1980.
Cakewalk. New York: Putnam, 1981.
Oral History. New York: Ballentine (pap.), 1984.
Family Linen. New York: Putnam, 1985.

Hendrie Jr., Don

Boomkitchwatt. Sante Fe: John Muir, 1973.
Scribble, Scribble, Scribble. Amherst: Lynx House, 1977.
Blount's Anvil. Amherst: Lynx House, 1980.

Wier, Allen

Blanco. Baton Rouge: Louisiana State University Press, 1978.
Things About to Disappear. Baton Rouge: Louisiana State University Press, 1978.
Departing as Air. New York: Simon and Schuster, 1983.